The Graceful Garden

A Jacobean Fantasy Quilt
By Denise Sheehan

The Graceful Garden

A Jacobean Fantasy Quilt
By Denise Sheehan

The Graceful Garden

A Jacobean Fantasy Quilt
By Denise Sheehan

EDITOR: Jenifer Dick

DESIGNER: Brian Grubb

PHOTOGRAPHY: Gregory Case Photography, Location
Aaron T. Leimkuehler, Studio
Additional Photography Mandy Sheehan

ILLUSTRATION: Eric Sears

TECHNICAL EDITOR: Nan Doljac

PRODUCTION ASSISTANCE: Jo Ann Groves

PUBLISHED BY:
Kansas City Star Books
1729 Grand Blvd.
Kansas City, Missouri, USA 64108

First edition, first printing
ISBN: 978-1-935362-08-1

Library of Congress Control Number: 2009923431

Printed in the United States of America by Walsworth Publishing Co., Marceline, MO

To order copies, call StarInfo at (816) 234-4636 and say "Books."

 KANSAS CITY STAR QUILTS
Continuing the Tradition

The Quilter's Home Page

www.PickleDish.com

ACKNOWLEDGEMENTS

This book never would have happened without the help and support of so many people. I will always be indebted to the following:

To The Kansas City Star Quilts staff: to Diane McLendon and Doug Weaver for asking me to write a book! To Jenifer Dick for your steady encouragement and patience. And to the fabulous team involved in editing, photographing, designing and illustrating this book.

To Paula Beatty and the Beatty family for your help and the opportunity to use your beautiful home and garden as the setting for this book. I feel so incredibly lucky.

To Gregory Case and Elena Morera for the on-site photography. Your sense of humor and persistence during a very long day is so appreciated.

To Mauna Wagner (and Jack, too) for the hours and hours you spent proofing and gently correcting. Your advice has been invaluable.

To Kristy Miller for your wonderful way with words.

To Kaaren Babb for brainstorming with me.

To Sophia Pearce, my Aussie friend, how lucky I am to have you come into my life at this moment in time. I am so thankful for your contribution and help with last minute details.

To Jean Deziak for your elegant embroidery.

To the Morning Threads ladies – we have been through births, marriages, graduations, divorce, hospital stays and sadly, death, together. As we've often said we provide each other with cheap therapy and the friendship and laughter we share is great medicine. Your support, encouragement and advice (asked for or not!) is greatly appreciated. Pam, Shirley, and Mauna, thank you for your last minute stitches.

To my quilters – Diana Johnson and Lynne Todoroff – you do such beautiful work!

To Lissa Alexander and Moda fabrics for so willingly providing beautiful fabrics to inspire my creativity.

To Nireko Ohira and the Lecien Corporation for providing the beautiful COSMO Embroidery Thread for stitching and embellishing.

To my beautiful daughter, Mandy, for the how-to photographs – you have a great future in front of you.

And last, but certainly not least, to my family and friends who understood – "sorry I have to work on the book!"

Thank you all!

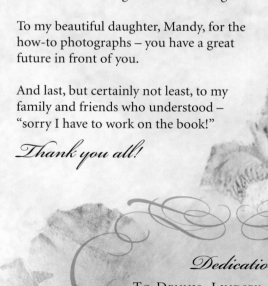

Dedication

TO DENNIS, LINDSEY AND MANDY

Contents

Introduction

A quilt is a simple thing; a top, a bottom and a layer wedged between. At the very least it is utilitarian, a covering used for warmth. At its best, it is a work of art, an historical marker, a unique use of fabric and thread that once ordinary becomes impressive.

If you were to see my quilts in chronological order you could mark my artistic phases. My early quilts were all pieced. I used traditional patterns and a limited palette. But, hungry for new ideas, I became a classaholic. Good teachers are so inspiring, and at one point I got nudged into trying appliqué. I loved how this ancient art of layering pieces of cloth opened up a whole new world of possibilities.

As a textile artist I love to thumb through books that have nothing to do with fabric. I am always on the hunt for "something" that I might be able to work into a quilt. Well, I thought, why not combine my pieced work with some appliqué? So I did, trying out different techniques, styles and combinations along the way.

The main quilt in this book, *The Graceful Garden* is the result of an assignment I was given in a design school class—paint a fabric pattern that was typical of the Jacobean period. I had no idea when or what Jacobean meant but it sounded elegant. I spent hours online and in the library researching the term and discovered numerous attributes that a Jacobean piece might include. Then I set out to create a one-dimensional design that could, in theory, become a fabric swatch.

WHAT IS JACOBEAN STYLE?

Jacobean refers to a style evident in the 16th and 17th Centuries. It was a form of embroidery that differed from the period norm in its use of fanciful flowers, meaty and meandering tree branches and an abundance of coiling tendrils crawling throughout the piece. Metal thread was used to embellish and provide an appearance of dimension, and the typical color range included muted hues of green and rose.

Well, as can happen, my initial research blossomed into a bigger idea. Certainly I could draw a picture for a quilt made up of all things Jacobean. How much more interesting it might be to design a quilt inspired by 16th Century women. As I researched further, my list of Jacobean traits increased to include multiple references to birds, a total disregard for proportion and an Asian influence on motifs. As you will notice, many of these Jacobean influences are evident in the patterns in this book.

The Graceful Garden, uses multiple layers of appliqué in many of its pieces. Mimicking the simple definition of a quilt, this use of building on layers and then finishing with embroidery adds movement and depth to the flora and fauna you will find in the pages that follow. The fanciful flowers have additional flowers embroidered within. Imaginative leaves twist and curl among the branches turning this quilt into a work of art.

ABOUT THE PHOTOGRAPHY

Historical perspective, I think, adds so much to our art. I truly enjoyed reading about the Jacobean period and marveled at how something old can be such an influence on something new. As you look at the pictures of the projects in this book, notice the setting in which they were taken. This yellow farmhouse, with its beautiful period décor, sits in the middle of suburban California on a piece of land originally owned by Dona Juana Sanchez de Pacheco, the widow of a Spanish explorer. The home was built in 1873, by a wealthy merchant. It was sold in 1903, and over the course of the

20th Century, became the home for eight different families. The house also boarded teachers who worked at the local school during the 1920s and 1930s.

Today this historic home is in the loving care of the Beatty family, who has lived there for almost 25 years. It, like a quilt, is a good reminder that life is a stack of layers. There is a top, a bottom and something wedged in between.

Have fun as you work with my patterns and

techniques but remember to look around you,

at the history that came before and let it influence

what you do and how you do it.

Starch Method Appliqué

I learned this method of appliqué years ago from a video by Pearl P. Periera of P3 Designs* in San Marcos, California. I have since modified her techniques to fit my needs.

MY FAVORITE SUPPLIES

Ironing pad

Craft iron

Mary Ellen's Best Press Starch*

Container for Starch

Roxanne's Glue Baste-it*

Aleene's Ok to Wash It glue*

Paper scissors

Small scissors with sharp point

Size 11 Straw Needles*

Stiletto

Small stencil paint brush

Thimble

Black permanent marker

YLI Silk Thread – neutrals*

Freezer Paper*

Rotary cutter with pinking blade

Light box

*See resources page 112 for more information.

PREPARING THE APPLIQUÉ SHAPES

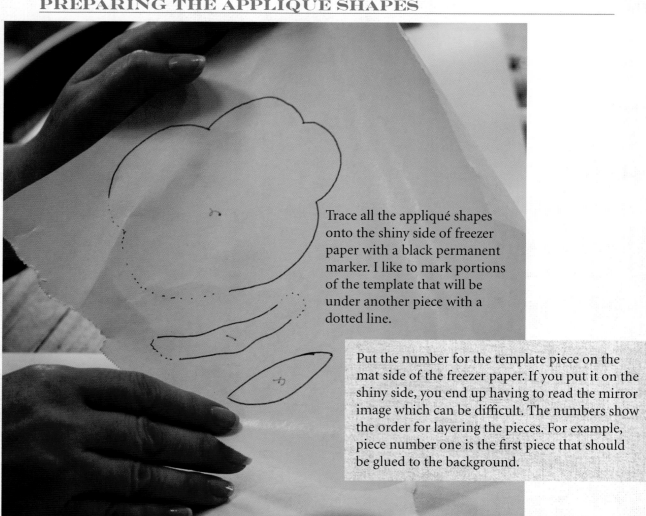

Trace all the appliqué shapes onto the shiny side of freezer paper with a black permanent marker. I like to mark portions of the template that will be under another piece with a dotted line.

Put the number for the template piece on the mat side of the freezer paper. If you put it on the shiny side, you end up having to read the mirror image which can be difficult. The numbers show the order for layering the pieces. For example, piece number one is the first piece that should be glued to the background.

Use a dry iron to press the traced templates on top of a second piece of freezer paper. (Ink should be in the middle of the two pieces of freezer paper to avoid transferring ink to your fabric. You should have your traced templates with the shiny side down on top of a blank piece of freezer paper with the shiny side down.) The freezer paper will stick to your ironing surface. Gently pull it off.

Cut out the shapes on the traced lines using paper scissors. It is important to cut a smooth edge to insure a smooth appliqué piece.

Iron the shiny side of the double thick freezer paper template to the wrong side of your fabric.

Cut out the shapes adding a scant 1/4" seam allowance around the freezer paper template.

Pour a small amount of liquid starch into a small container. You can use regular spray starch by spraying a little starch into a small container. It will be foamy at first, but will turn to liquid after a few minutes.

Place the appliqué shape, fabric side down, on your ironing pad (the freezer paper template is still attached).

Using a small stencil brush, wet the 1/4" seam allowance with liquid starch.

Note: It is important to iron in the same direction that you sew. I am right-handed and iron counter clockwise, the same way that I sew. If you are left-handed, you should prepare clockwise assuming you sew clockwise. This is important for the points on your appliqué shapes.

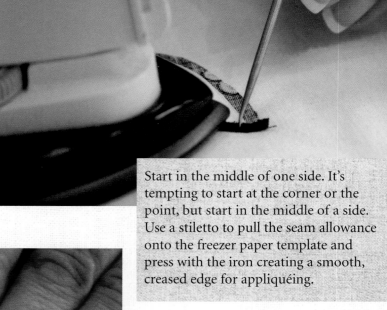

Start in the middle of one side. It's tempting to start at the corner or the point, but start in the middle of a side. Use a stiletto to pull the seam allowance onto the freezer paper template and press with the iron creating a smooth, creased edge for appliquéing.

For the first side of the point, continue pressing to the end of the fabric. For the next side, turn the piece around and continue pressing down the next side.

This creates a little flag at the point. If you sew counter-clockwise, your flag should be on the left side of your pieces as you look at the template. If you sew clockwise, your flag should be on the right side of your piece. Both of these photos show the flag for sewing counter-clockwise.

If you have an inside point or a tight inside curve, clip to within 1-2 threads of the freezer paper.

There is no need to turn under the fabric where you marked the template with a dotted line (this edge will be hidden by another piece of fabric).

When you have completed your shape, turn the shape over, press lightly with iron and remove the freezer paper.

Cut your appliqué background over-sized using the pinked edge rotary cutter to help prevent fraying. Place your complete pattern under the background to use as your placement guide. A light box is helpful.

Using a thin line of glue, glue-baste your shapes in place. Leave the flag area of a point free of glue so that you can turn under the flag (see above).

Stitch pieces to background. Start by coming up from underneath the background right in or as close as possible to the crease. Your next stitch will start slightly under the appliqué piece and come up right in, or as close as possible, to the crease.

For inside points, as you sew, you can use a toothpick to put a small dot of the Aleene's glue right at the point. Use your needle to ease threads into and under the glue.

For outside points, as you stitch toward the point, make your stitches closer together. Take an extra stitch right in the point.

Trim the point parallel with the seam allowance you just finished.

Denise's Details:
Sometimes the flags at the points can fray as you turn them. Moistening the flag helps with the fraying. Don't tell anyone, but I just touch the flag with my tongue!

Stab the flag with your needle. Turn the point of the flag under itself as you push it under the appliqué piece. Hold it under with your thumb as you stitch it closed.

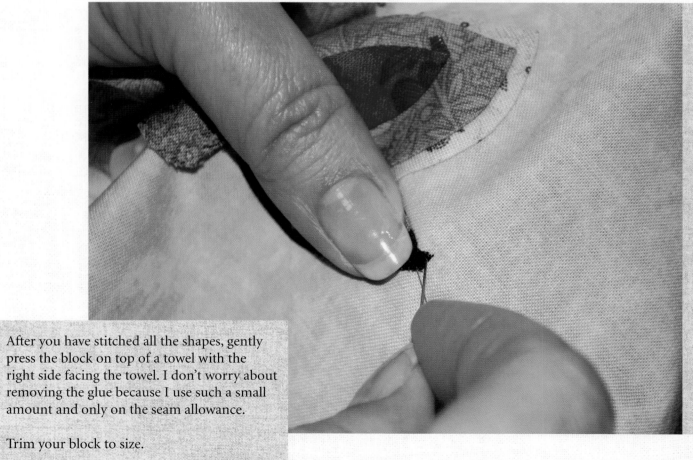

After you have stitched all the shapes, gently press the block on top of a towel with the right side facing the towel. I don't worry about removing the glue because I use such a small amount and only on the seam allowance.

Trim your block to size.

Embroidery Instructions

These are very basic stitching instructions. If you need more detailed information, there are lots of great embroidery reference books available at your local quilt shop or library.

SUPPLIES

#11 Embroidery Needle
Embroidery floss—I use COSMO brand. (See resources on page 112.) Or use your favorite brand.

Separate the strands of embroidery floss. I like to use two strands at a time. Thread the needle with two strands. Knot the end and you're ready to go.

FRENCH KNOT

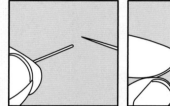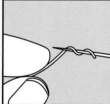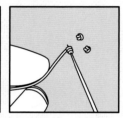

1. Bring the floss up through the fabric.
2. Hold the floss with your left hand and the needle with your right hand (assuming you're right handed).
3. Wrap the floss around the needle 2-3 times.
4. Put the needle back down into the fabric right next to the where the needle came up.
5. Slide the knot down the needle, holding floss taut.
6. Hold the knot in place under your thumb and push the needle through the fabric.

LAZY DAISY

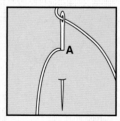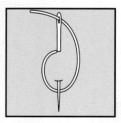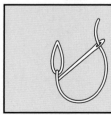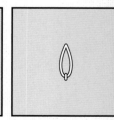

1. Bring needle up at A. Make a loop with your floss and put needle back in at A. Bring the needle point back out at the top of the lazy daisy.
2. Pull floss through gently with the top of the loop under the point of the needle.
3. Continue pulling on the floss until you have the loop shape desired.
4. Complete the stitch over the top of the loop.

BLANKET STITCH

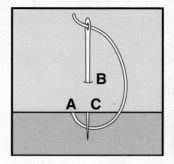 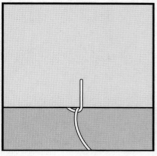 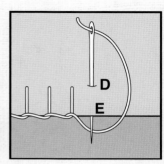 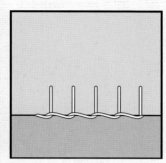

1. Start with your floss anchored underneath the fabric. Bring the floss out at A and down into the fabric at B. Bring the floss out underneath the fabric at C. The floss is underneath the point of the needle.
2. Pull the floss until the stitch sits against the edge of the fabric.
3. Take the needle down at D and up at E with the floss under the point of the needle.
4. Continue taking even stitches.

OUTLINE STITCH

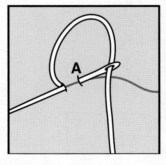 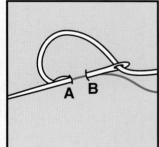 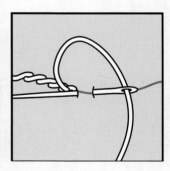 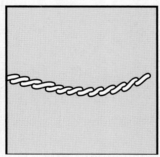

1. Bring needle up from underneath fabric and down at A. The needle comes back up where the floss first came out of the fabric. Keep the floss above the needle. The next stitch will go down at B and come back up at A.
2. Continue taking even stitches with the point of the needle always coming up where the last stitch went down and keeping the floss above the needle.

The Graceful Garden

49 1/2" X 61 1/2"

Quilt made by Denise Sheehan
Quilted by Diana Johnson,
San Leandro, California

The Graceful Garden quilt is composed of 12 different blocks. Three blocks are repeated: sashing strips, squares and checkerboards are added to complete the top.

To make your Graceful Garden quilt, pick your color palette first. When you are working on an appliqué block, prepare the block, put it up on your design wall, step back, squint your eyes and decide if you like what you see. Now is the time to make any changes. Is there enough contrast between your fabrics? If you're not happy with a fabric, try a different one. That's the beauty of the starch method of appliqué. You can see the project before you start sewing and it's easy to make changes. I love to focus on the motifs in fabric. Often when I'm placing a template on the fabric, I will center it over a specific part of the fabric to showcase the motif, color, texture or tiny detail in the fabric.

SUPPLIES

Based on 42" wide fabric.

To make The Graceful Garden quilt, you will need to collect the following fabrics:

12 fat quarters of cream, light blue, light tan for backgrounds

3/8 yard cream for Block No. 11 The Garden Maze background

17-20 fat quarters of browns—include different values, floral prints, bird fabrics and geometrics

10 fat quarters of pinks and reds

10 fat quarters of blues

5 fat quarters of tan

3 yards for backing
1/2 yard for binding

> *Denise's Details:*
> Because I like to use a large variety of fabrics, I have over-estimated the yardage on all the colors with the exception of the backgrounds. You can often use scraps from your stash for the appliqué pieces

MAKING THE BLOCKS

Individual instructions for each block begin on page 24. Once all the blocks are made and trimmed to the correct size, use the following quilt top assembly instructions to finish the quilt.

PREPARING THE APPLIQUÉ BLOCKS

The appliqué templates for each block begin on page 82. The Dahlia, Magnolia Branch and Rose blocks are separated out into sections over several pages. You'll need to trace or copy them each onto one large piece of paper using the registration guides to line them up properly to make the full-size template.

You will then need to make individual freezer paper templates for each shape as described in the Starch Method Appliqué section on page 10.

For embroidering on the appliqué blocks, transfer the embroidery lines to the individual pieces before you start layering them together. Use a size 11 embroidery needle and 2 strands of your favorite floss for the stitching. On the appliqué templates, the dashed lines represent the embroidery placement.

Quilt Top Assembly Diagram

ASSEMBLING THE QUILT TOP

The quilt is assembled in four sections. I highly recommend using a design wall and cutting your sashing and border strips as you go. I found that I needed to audition fabrics to make sure the strips complemented the blocks and didn't overpower them.

> *Denise's Details:*
> A design wall is invaluable. My design wall is made from a piece of flannel I pin over a quilt that hangs on the wall. If you can't find wall space, use a large piece of foam core (found at most art supply stores) covered with flannel.

SUPPLIES

From the supplies listed on page 19, choose
8-10 fat quarters of blues, tans, pinks, browns for sashing strips
8-10 fat quarters of browns for borders

SECTION 1

Section 1 consists of the Dahlia, Garden Steps, Poppy, Hydrangea, Whirligig and Garden Maze blocks.

Cut 2 – 2 1/2" x 16 1/2" sashing strips.

Stitch 1 sashing strip to the bottom of the Dahlia block.

Stitch the Garden Steps block to a Poppy block.

Stitch one of the Hydrangea blocks to a Whirligig block.

Stitch these 2 units together and add to the Dahlia/sashing unit as shown in the diagram.

Stitch the remaining sashing strip to the top of the Garden Maze block and add to the unit above.

SECTION 2

Section 2 consists of a Checkerboard unit and the Hydrangea, Courtyard, Whirligig and Magnolia Branch blocks.

Checkerboard

Cut 1 – 1 1/2" x 19" strip of blue fabric.
Cut 1 – 1 1/2" x 19" strip of tan fabric.
Cut 1 – 1 1/2" x 7" strip of blue fabric.
Cut 1 – 1 1/2" x 7" strip of tan fabric.

Stitch the 2 long strips together as shown in the diagram below. Press the seam toward the blue fabric. Cross cut the strip set into 12 – 1 1/2" pieces. Assemble the pieces into a checkerboard unit as shown.

Stitch the 2 short strips together. Press the seam toward the blue fabric. Cross cut the strip set into 4 – 1 1/2" units. Assemble the pieces into two four-patch units. Reserve these for Sections 3 and 4.

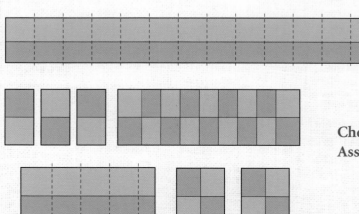

Checkerboard Assembly

TO ASSEMBLE SECTION 2:

Cut 1 – 2 1/2" x 12 1/2" sashing strip.

Fussy cut 4 – 4 1/2" squares of floral or bird fabric focusing on a motif. Reserve 2 of the squares for Section 3.

Stitch 2 of the fussy cut squares together. Stitch this unit to the bottom of the remaining Hydrangea block.

Stitch the long checkerboard strip to left side of the Hydrangea unit.

Stitch the Courtyard block to the right side of the Hydrangea unit. Stitch the sashing strip to the right side of the Courtyard block.

Stitch the remaining Whirligig block to the left side of the Magnolia Branch block. Stitch to the bottom of the Hydrangea/Courtyard unit.

SECTION 3

Section 3 consists of the Tulip and Flagstone blocks.

Cut 1 – 2 1/2" x 10 1/2" sashing strip.
Cut 1 – 2 1/2" x 14 1/2" sashing strip.
Cut 1 – 2 1/2" x 22 1/2" sashing strip. You may have to piece two strips together to get the correct length.

Stitch the 2 reserved 4 1/2" squares together. Stitch this unit to the bottom of the Tulip block.

Stitch one of the reserved checkerboard four-patch units to the end of a 2 1/2" x 10 1/2" sashing strip. Stitch to the right side of the Tulip unit. Add the Flagstone block to the right.

Stitch a 2 1/2" x 22 1/2" sashing strip to the top of the Tulip/Flagstone unit.

Stitch a 2 1/2" x 14 1/2" sashing strip to the left of the Tulip/Flagstone unit.

Stitch Section 3 to the bottom of Section 2.

SECTION 4

Section 4 consists of the Iris, Mirror Image Poppy and Rose blocks.

Cut1 – 2 1/2" x 14 1/2" sashing strips.

Cut 1 – 2 1/2" x 8 1/2" sashing strip.

Stitch a 2 1/2" x 8 1/2" sashing unit to the bottom of the Iris block. Add a Poppy block to the bottom of the Iris unit.

Stitch the remaining checkerboard four-patch unit to the end of the 2 1/2" x 14 1/2" sashing strip. Stitch to the top of the Rose block with the four-patch unit on the left side.

Stitch the Rose unit to the Iris/Poppy unit.

Finishing the top

Stitch Section 4 to the bottom of Section 3.

Stitch the Section 2/3/4 unit to Section 1.

BORDERS

The borders are made of a variety of brown fabrics. Before cutting the browns, fold them to the approximate size of the border segments and audition them on your design wall. Decide now if they complement the quilt or should be changed out.

Fussy cut 4 – 5 1/4" squares of floral or bird fabric for the cornerstones centering on a motif. I used four birds for my cornerstones.

Left border
Cut the following pieces from the brown fabrics and stitch them together in the order given starting from the top:
5 1/4" x 11 1/2"
5 1/4" x 11 1/2"
5 1/4" x 6 1/2"
5 1/4" x 11 1/2"
5 1/4" x 5 1/2"
5 1/4" x 8 1/2"
Stitch to the left side of the quilt top.

Right border
Cut the following pieces and stitch them together in the order given starting from the top:
5 1/4" x 14 1/2"
5 1/4" x 10 1/2"
5 1/4" x 5 1/2"
5 1/4" x 10 1/2"
5 1/4" x 13 1/2"
Stitch to the right side of the quilt top.

Top border
Cut the following pieces and stitch them together in the order given:
5 1/4" x 10 1/2"
5 1/4" x 14 1/2"
5 1/4" x 6 1/2"
5 1/4" x 10 1/2"
Add a fussy cut cornerstone to each end of the top border.
Stitch top border to the quilt top.

Bottom border
Cut the following pieces and stitch them together in the order given:
5 1/4" x 6 1/2"
5 1/4" x 12 1/2"
5 1/4" x 8 1/2"
5 1/4" x 5 1/2"
5 1/4" x 9 1/2"
Add a fussy cut cornerstone to each end of the bottom border.

Stitch bottom border to the quilt top.

FINISHING THE QUILT

Layer backing, batting and top.
Quilt as desired and bind.

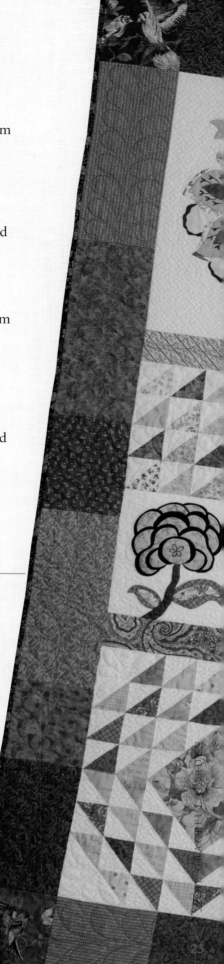

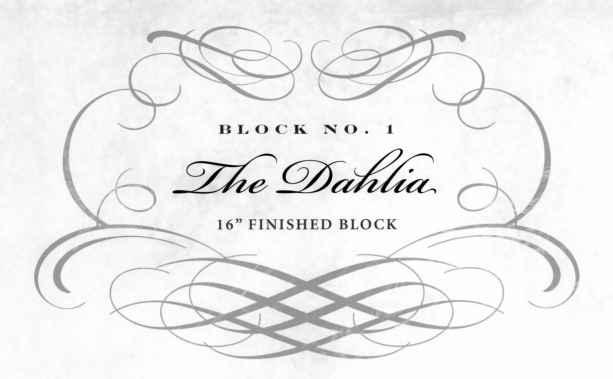

BLOCK NO. 1

The Dahlia

16" FINISHED BLOCK

This is the first and the most intricate block, but don't let that daunt you! Take your time and enjoy the process. If you're creating this quilt as a block of the month, don't rush the stitching. There will be months where you will have only piecing to do and it will be nice to return to this block for some handwork.

SUPPLIES

For the background:
1 fat quarter cream, light blue or light tan

For the appliqué:
4 fat quarters of blues
6-11 fat quarters of different values of browns
2 fat quarters of pinks/reds

For the embroidery:
Brown, pink and red embroidery floss

CUTTING

From the background fabric, cut 1 – 17" square.

TECHNIQUE

Appliqué: The templates are on pages 83-87.

Embroidery: Use 2 strands of floss and stitch using the Outline stitch for the lines and the Lazy Daisy stitch for the petal shapes.

FINISHING

Trim the block to 16 1/2" square.

> *Denise's Details:*
> When transferring lines for embroidery, if you will be using a Lazy Daisy stitch, just mark dots where the stitch will go. The stitch can be lazy and doesn't always sit perfectly!

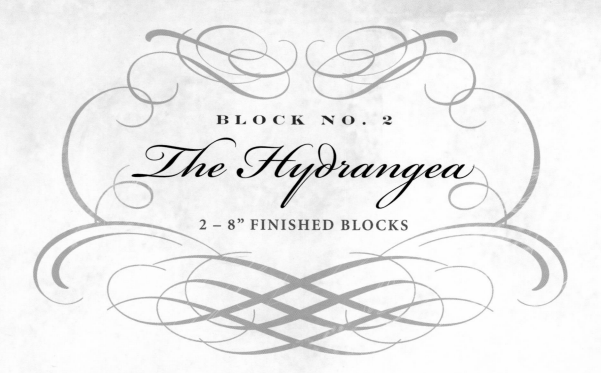

The Hydrangea

This block appears twice in the quilt. They have many pieces and the preparation takes a little time, but they are very easy shapes to stitch. You'll be amazed at how quickly you will finish these two hydrangeas.

SUPPLIES

For the backgrounds:
2 fat quarters of cream, light blue or light tan

For the appliqué:
5 fat quarters of browns
2 fat quarters of blues
3 fat quarters of pinks

For the embroidery:
Dark pink, red, or brown embroidery floss

CUTTING

From the background fabrics, cut 2 – 9" squares.

TECHNIQUE

Appliqué: The template is on page 82.

Embroidery: Use 2 strands of floss and stitch using the Outline stitch on the center circle and single straight stitches on the flower petals.

FINISHING

Trim each block to 8 1/2" square.

THE GRACEFUL GARDE

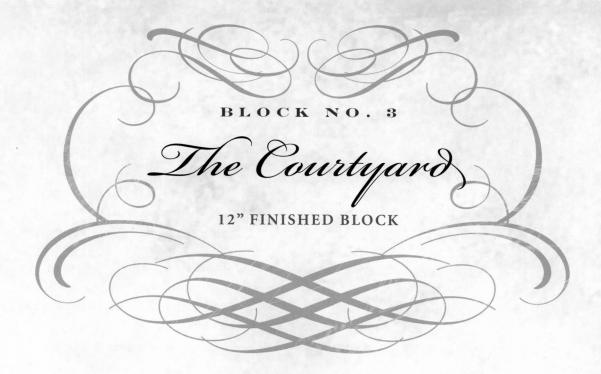

BLOCK NO. 3

The Courtyard

12" FINISHED BLOCK

This block goes together in a snap with the help of a quick method for creating half-square triangles and a few flying geese. You will use this half-square triangle technique often throughout the quilt.

SUPPLIES

1 fat quarter pale blue for the background
1 fat quarter dark brown floral
1 fat quarter dark brown geometric
1 fat quarter blue floral
1 fat quarter light brown floral

CUTTING

From the pale blue background:
cut 2 – 4 7/8" squares. Cut each of these once diagonally for a total of 4 (A) triangles.

cut 10 – 2 7/8" squares. Cut 8 of these once diagonally for a total of 16 (B) triangles and 2 (B) squares.

From the dark brown floral
(outside triangles):
cut 4 – 2 7/8" squares. Cut each of these once diagonally for a total of 8 (C) triangles.

From the dark brown geometric
(middle triangles):
cut 2 – 2 7/8" squares (D).
cut 1 – 5 1/4" square. Cut the square twice diagonally for a total of 4 (E) triangles.

From the blue floral (center triangles):
cut 1 – 4 7/8" square. Cut the square once diagonally for a total of 2 (F) triangles.

From the light brown floral
(center triangles):
cut 1 – 4 7/8" square. Cut the square once diagonally for a total of 2 (G) triangles.

PIECING

Center

Sew an F triangle to a
G triangle.
Press towards F.

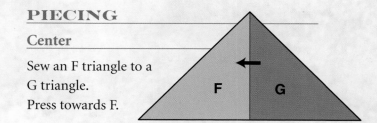

Denise's Details:
Handle squares cut diagonally with care. The bias edge will stretch easily!

Repeat and sew the two units together as shown in the diagram. Pressing in the direction of the arrows. The center should measure 8 1/2" square.

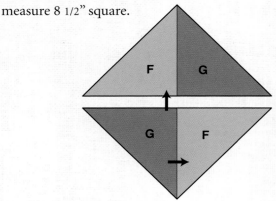

Half-square triangle units

Draw a diagonal line from corner to corner on the wrong side of two B squares. With right sides together, layer a B square on top of a D square. (See the Diagram Step 1)

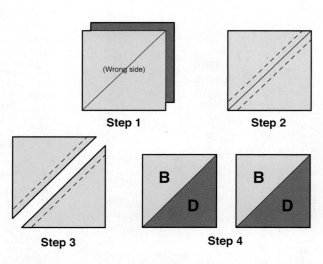

Step 1

Step 2

Step 3

Step 4

Stitch 1/4" from each side of the drawn line. (Step 2)

Cut apart on the marked line. (Step 3) Press towards D. (Step 4) The half-square triangle units should measure 2 1/2" square. Repeat for a total of 4 – 2 1/2" half square triangle units.

Inside Corners

Stitch two B triangles to each side of the half-square triangle unit as shown in the diagram. Repeat for a total of four corner units.

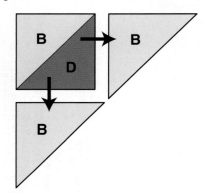

Finger press the Inside Corner units in half to find the centers. Finger press the Center unit in half to find the centers. Matching the centers, stitch two Inside Corner units to the opposite sides of the Center unit.

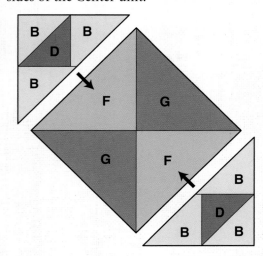

Add the remaining two corners as shown in the diagram.

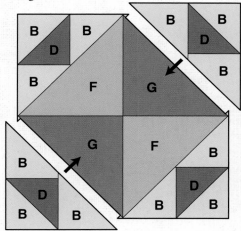

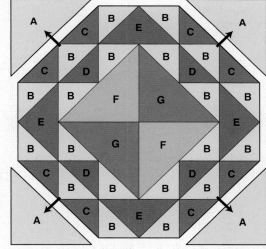

Repeat on the remaining flying geese. Finger press the flying geese units to find the center. Stitch the flying geese units to the top and bottom of the center square matching centers. Add the right and left sides.

Flying Geese units

With the right sides together line up the bottom edge of a B triangle to the long side of an E triangle as shown in the diagram.

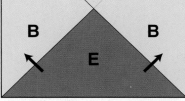

Stitch and press towards the background. Repeat on the opposite side.

Stitch the A triangles to the block. The block should measure 12 1/2".

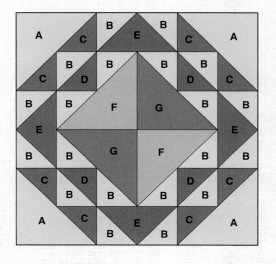

Repeat for a total of four Flying Geese. The Flying Geese should measure 2 1/2" x 4 1/2".

Stitch C triangles on the sides of flying geese as shown in the diagram.

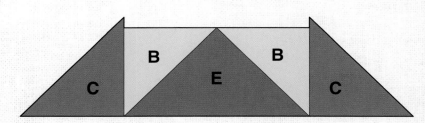

Add some fun to your garden with a new arrangement of half-square triangles. You can visualize these Whirligigs spinning in the breeze.

SUPPLIES

For block No. 1
1 fat quarter of cream tone on tone
1 fat quarter of red
1 fat quarter of brown paisley
1 fat quarter of light brown

For block No. 2
1 fat quarter of cream (you can use the same fat quarter from above)
1 fat quarter of tan
1 fat quarter of blue
1 fat quarter of pink

CUTTING

From both the cream for the first block and cream for the second block (background):
cut 6 – 2 7/8" squares from each fat quarter (12 squares total).

From the red for the first block and tan for the second block (outside triangles):
cut 4 – 2 7/8" squares from each fat quarter.

From the brown paisley for the first block and blue for the second block (spokes of whirligig):
cut 4 – 2 7/8" squares from each fat quarter.

From the light brown for the first block and pink for the second block (center square):
cut 2 – 2 7/8" squares from each fat quarter.

PIECING

Half-square triangles (refer to page 32 for diagrams)

Draw a diagonal line from corner to corner on the wrong side of each cream square and each light brown square.

Cream and red half-square triangles

With right sides together, layer a cream square on top of each red square.
Stitch 1/4" from each side of the drawn lines.
Cut apart on the marked lines.
Press towards the red. The half-square triangle units (8) should measure 2 1/2" square

Cream and brown paisley half-square triangles

With right sides together, layer a cream square on top of each of two brown paisley squares.
Stitch 1/4" from each side of the drawn lines.
Cut the squares apart on the marked lines.
Press towards the paisley. The half-square triangle units (4) should measure 2 1/2" square.

Light brown and brown
paisley half-square triangles

With right sides together, layer a light brown square on top of each of two brown paisley squares. Stitch 1/4" from each side of drawn lines. Cut apart on the marked lines. Press towards the paisley. The half-square triangle units (4) should measure 2 1/2" square.

BLOCK ASSEMBLY

Sew the half-square triangle units into rows as shown in the diagram. Press in the direction of the arrows. Sew the rows together. The block should measure 8 1/2".

For the second block:
Repeat the instructions above for the second Whirligig block. You will be making cream and tan, cream and blue, and blue and pink half-square triangles.

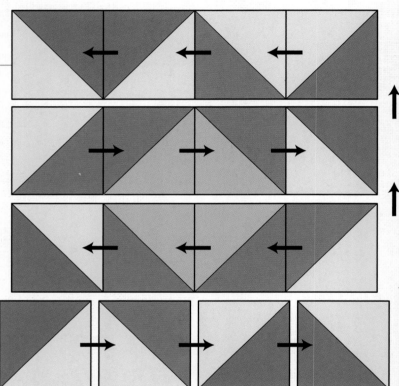

> *Denise's Details:*
> If you don't want to draw diagonal lines, use a piece of masking tape on the bed of your sewing machine. Draw three lines on the tape, one in line with the needle and one 1/4" on either side of the center line. Use the lines to guide your squares as you sew.

BLOCK NO. 5

The Magnolia Branch

8" x 16" FINISHED BLOCK

Meandering tree branches combine with fanciful flowers in this block. Large, gently curving shapes make this block easy to appliqué.

SUPPLIES

For the background:
1 fat quarter cream, light blue or light tan

For the appliqué:
6 fat quarters of browns
2 fat quarters of blues
1 fat quarter of red

For the embroidery:
Cream embroidery floss

CUTTING

From the background fabric, cut 1 – 9" x 17" rectangle.

TECHNIQUE

Appliqué: The templates are on pages 88-89.

Embroidery: Use 2 strands of floss and stitch using the Outline stitch and the Lazy Daisy stitch.

FINISHING

Trim the block to 8 1/2" x 16 1/2".

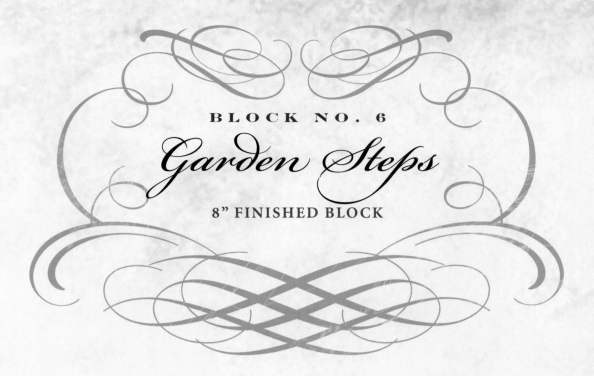

Garden Steps

8" FINISHED BLOCK

Use a variety of colors to create these garden steps. A different technique is used to construct these half-square triangles.

SUPPLIES

1 fat quarter of cream fabric
16 – 2 7/8" squares of assorted tan, brown and blue fabrics

CUTTING

From the background fabric:

cut 8 – 2 7/8" squares. Cut each of these once diagonally.

From the assorted tans, browns and blues:

cut 8 to 16 – 2 7/8" squares. Cut each of these once diagonally.

PIECING

Match a background triangle with a tan, brown or blue triangle, right sides together. Stitch as shown in the diagram. Press away from the background. Repeat for a total of 16 – 2 1/2" half-square triangles.

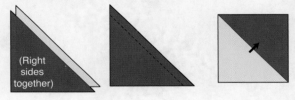

(Right sides together)

BLOCK ASSEMBLY

Stitch the half-square triangles into four rows of four. Press in the direction of arrows.

Stitch the rows together. The block should measure 8 1/2".

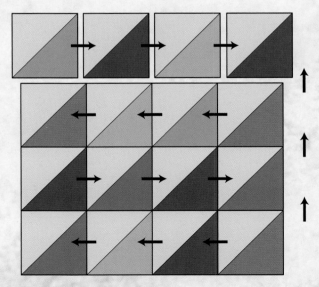

Denise's Details:

If you like the look of having no repeats, cut 16 squares of the colored fabrics and cut each in half diagonally. Use only one triangle from each fabric for your block. Keep in mind, this will leave you with many leftover triangles.

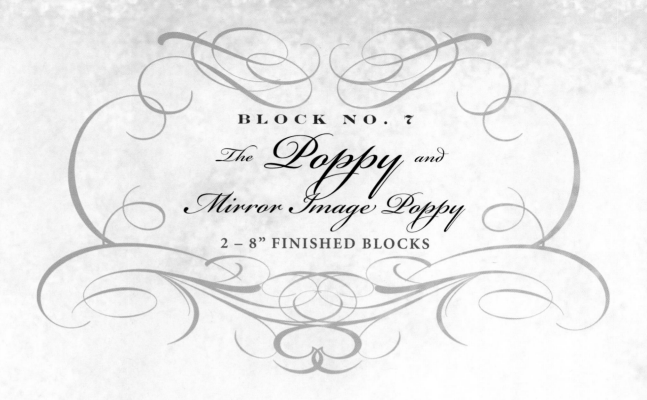

BLOCK NO. 7

The **Poppy** *and*
Mirror Image Poppy

2 – 8" FINISHED BLOCKS

These fantasy flowers have coiling tendrils in the form of embroidery. Tiny stitches are the secret to the tight coils. You will have the opportunity to practice your points on the many layered leaves of these blocks.

SUPPLIES

For the background:
2 fat quarters cream, light blue or light tan

For the appliqué:
8 fat quarters of browns
4 fat quarters of tan
1 fat quarter of blue
1 fat quarter of pink

For the embroidery:
Dark pink/red, brown and blue embroidery floss

CUTTING

From the background fabric, cut 2 – 9" squares.

TECHNIQUE

Appliqué: The templates are on pages 90-91.

Embroidery: Use 2 strands of floss and stitch using the Outline stitch.

FINISHING

Trim each block to 8 1/2" square.

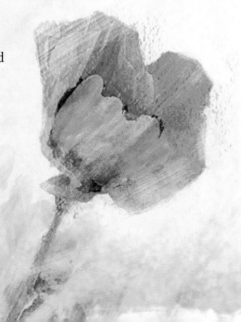

BLOCK NO. 8

The Tulip

8" FINISHED BLOCK

Here is a quick appliqué block. Only 10 large pieces and a little embroidery make up this sweet block.

SUPPLIES

For the background:
1 fat quarter cream

For the appliqué:
3 fat quarters of browns
3 fat quarters of pinks/red

For the embroidery:
Dark brown embroidery floss

CUTTING

From the background fabric, cut 1 – 9" square.

TECHNIQUE

Appliqué: The template is on page 92.

Embroidery: Use 2 strands of floss and stitch using the Outline stitch.

FINISHING

Trim the block to 8 1/2" square.

BLOCK NO. 9

The Flagstone

12" FINISHED BLOCK

This is a great block to highlight pretty floral prints or a large print. If you're making this quilt as a block of the month, this is a good month to catch up on any appliqué you have waiting.

SUPPLIES

9 different floral prints measuring larger than 4 1/2" square

1 fat quarter of dark brown

CUTTING

From 9 different floral prints: cut 1 – 4 1/2" square from each floral.

From the dark brown: cut 36 – 1 1/4" squares.

PIECING

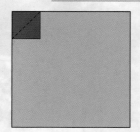

With right sides together, align a dark brown square on the corner of a floral square. Stitch diagonally from corner to corner as shown in the diagram.

Repeat on the remaining three corners of the floral square.

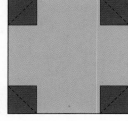

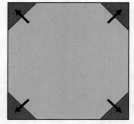

Press the corners out. Trim the middle brown layer.

Repeat with the remaining 8 floral squares and brown squares. Sew the squares together in three rows of three as shown in the diagram. Press in the direction of the arrows. Stitch the rows together. The block should measure 12 1/2" square.

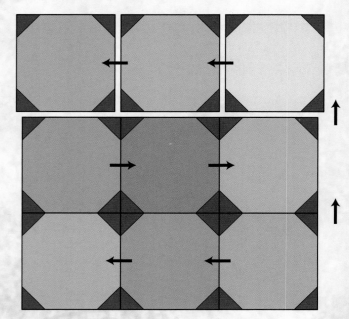

Denise's Details:

To add a corner triangle, follow these steps: Layer on a corner square, sew on the diagonal, press the corner square out to form a corner triangle, and trim. Trimming only the middle layer will help stabilize the original shape – in this case the 4 1/2" square.

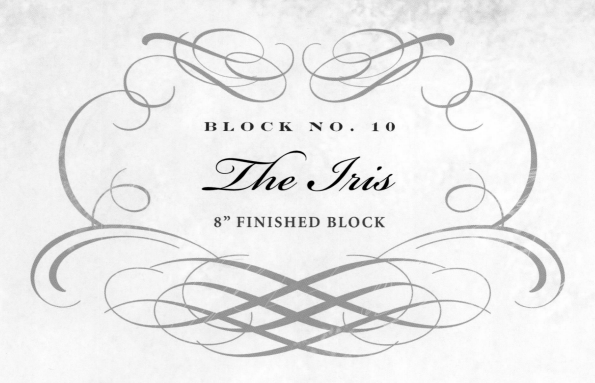

BLOCK NO. 10

The Iris

8" FINISHED BLOCK

The Iris block with its down-turned petals is a garden favorite.

SUPPLIES

For the background:
1 fat quarter cream

For the appliqué:
3 fat quarters of browns
1 fat quarter of blue
1 fat quarter of red

For the embroidery:
Cream embroidery floss

CUTTING

From the background fabric, cut 1 – 9" square.

TECHNIQUE

Appliqué: The template is on page 93.

Embroidery: Use 2 strands of floss and stitch using the Outline stitch.

FINISHING

Trim the block to 8 1/2" square.

BLOCK NO. 11

The Garden Maze

16" FINISHED BLOCK

Stroll along and create your garden maze as you wind your way to the center flower.

SUPPLIES

3/8 yard of cream background fabric
1 fat quarter of large floral print
12 fat quarters of assorted pinks, red, tans and browns

CUTTING

From the large floral:
cut 1 – 6 1/8" square.

From the cream background:
cut 2 – 4 7/8" squares. Cut each of these once diagonally for a total of 4 large triangles.

cut 24 – 2 7/8" squares. Cut 4 of these once diagonally for a total of 8 small triangles and 20 squares.

From the 12 assorted pinks, red, tans and browns:
cut 2 – 2 7/8" squares from each of 12 fabrics for a total of 24 squares. Cut 4 of these once diagonally for a total of 8 triangles and 20 squares.

PIECING

Half-square triangles

Draw a diagonal line from corner to corner on the wrong side of cream background squares. With right sides together, layer a background square on top of one of the pink, red, tan or brown (colored) squares. (See diagram step 1) Stitch 1/4" from each side of the drawn line. (Step 2)

Cut apart on the marked line. (Step 3)
Press towards the colored square. (Step 4)

Repeat for a total of 40 – 2 1/2" half-square triangles.

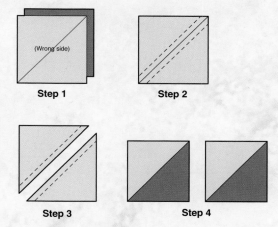

Step 1   Step 2

Step 3   Step 4

Corner units

Stitch a small background triangle to the adjacent sides of a half-square triangle as shown in the diagram. Press the seams toward the background triangles. Repeat for a total of four corner units.

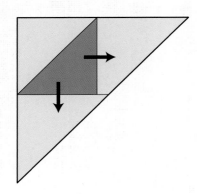

Finger press the large floral square in half to find the centers. Stitch the corner units to opposite sides of the large floral square matching the centers. Press the seams towards the square. Add the corner units to the remaining sides. Press the seams towards the square.

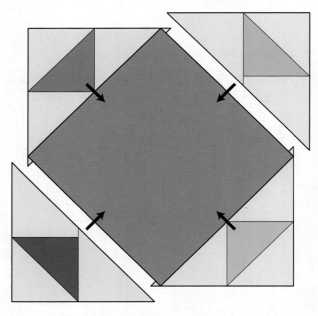

BLOCK ASSEMBLY

Lay out the block arranging the half-square triangles and remaining colored triangles in a pleasing manner.

Row 1: Stitch four half-square triangles together pressing in the direction of arrows. Add a colored triangle to both ends of the row as shown in the diagram. Repeat for row 8.

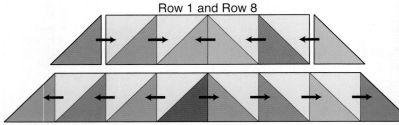

Row 1 and Row 8

Row 2 and Row 7

Row 2: Stitch six half-square triangles together pressing in the direction of arrows. Add a colored triangle to both ends of the row as shown in the diagram. Repeat for row 7.

Stitch rows 1 and 2 together for the top unit. Stitch rows 7 and 8 together for the bottom unit.

Side Units: Stitch two vertical rows with four half-square triangles in each. Stitch the rows together. Repeat for the opposite side.

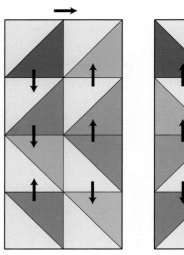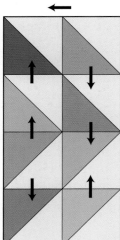

Stitch the side units to the center.
Stitch the top and bottom units to
the center.

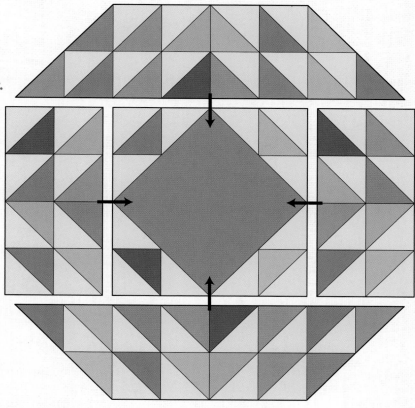

**Stitch the large background
triangles to the block.**
The block should measure 16 1/2" square.

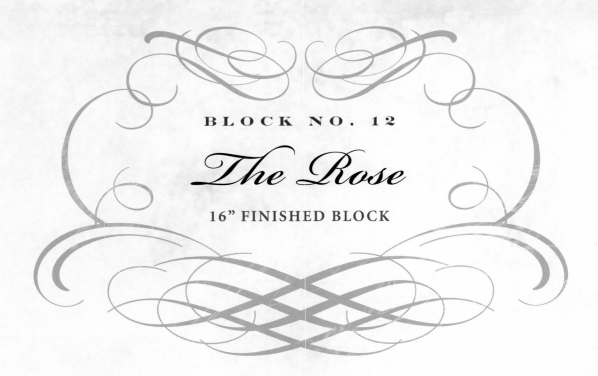

BLOCK NO. 12

The Rose

16" FINISHED BLOCK

What would a garden be without a rose? Enjoy the intricate appliqué and embroidery of the final block.

SUPPLIES

For the background:
1 fat quarter cream, light blue or light tan

For the appliqué:
10 fat quarters of browns
2 fat quarters of tan
4 fat quarters of pinks/red
4 fat quarters of blues

For the embroidery:
Blue embroidery floss

CUTTING

From the background fabric, cut 1 – 17" square.

TECHNIQUE

Appliqué: The templates are on pages 94-98.

Embroidery: Use 2 strands of floss and stitch using the Outline stitch.

> *Denise's Details:*
> I chose not to embroider the little flowers inside the rose buds. The fabric I used was patterned and I fussy cut the fabric to show the flowers in the fabric.

FINISHING

Trim the block to 16 1/2" square.

Petite Dahlia Pincushion

6" DIAMETER

Made by Denise Sheehan, Lafayette, California

Who wouldn't love to have this cute little pincushion sitting next to the sewing machine? The Dahlia block inspired this flower. I found the cute vintage button at a local antique store. The stuffing for the pincushion is walnut hulls which I found at a feed store.

SUPPLIES

9 1/2" square of blue wool for top circle
9 1/2" square of green wool for bottom circle
6" square of dark pink wool for large flower
5 1/2" square of light pink wool for small flower
Vintage button
Pink and blue embroidery floss
1" strip of batting approximately 19 1/2" long
Walnut hulls, polyester fiberfill or kitty litter for filling
Funnel
Long Needle
Freezer Paper

> *Denise's Details:*
> If your wool is loosely woven you can try felting it by getting it very wet (or machine wash) and machine drying it.

Trace the templates found on pages 60-61 onto freezer paper. Iron the freezer paper templates onto wool. Cut out the shapes following the freezer paper templates. There is no need to add a seam allowance.

Use three strands of embroidery floss for this project. Finish the edges of the flower shapes with a blanket stitch. See embroidery instructions on page 17.

Stitch the circles together with blanket stitch leaving about two inches open. Use the 1" strip of batting to line the inside seam line. Use a funnel to stuff the pincushion with filling. Stitch the opening closed with blanket stitch.

Using a long needle, stitch up and down through the center of the pincushion three to four times pulling the thread as tight as possible each time to create an indentation. Take a stitch up from the center, over the side of the pincushion and back up through the center pulling the thread as tight as possible. Take the next stitch to the opposite side and back up through the center. You've now divided the circle in half. Continue taking stitches over the side and back through the center dividing the circle into fourths and then into eighths.

Join the large flower and the small flower, rotating the petals in the small flower to alternate with the petals in the large flower. Then add the button and stitch through all three. Attach the flowers and button to the circles with a couple of stitches through the center.

Petite Dahlia
Pincushion Template
6" DIAMETER

Sophia's Field of Greens

56 1/2" X 57 1/2"

Made by Sophia Pearce, San Francisco, California
Quilted by Diana Johnson, San Leandro, California

Sophia is a young friend I met in design class. She is originally from Tasmania, Australia and currently resides in San Francisco. When I found out she was a quilter, I asked if she would design a quilt for this book. This beautiful quilt is jelly roll friendly.

SUPPLIES

18-20 fat quarters or 2 jelly rolls blues and greens
1/4 yard green for border fabric
1/2 yard for binding
3 1/2 yards for backing

CUTTING

From the fat quarters:
Cut 2 1/2" wide strips (if you are using jelly rolls, skip this step). Using the template or a 60 degree triangle ruler, cut strips into triangles. You will need 1,392 triangles.

From the border fabric:
Cut 6 – 3/4" strips from the width of the fabric.

From the binding fabric:
Cut 6 – 2 1/4" strips from the width of the fabric.

> *Denise's Details:*
> This quilt involves a lot of bias edges. Be very gentle when handling it to avoid stretching.

ASSEMBLY

Stitch individual triangles into sets of two.
Press the seams open.

Stitch the pairs into sets of four.
Using a design wall or large space, arrange the sets of four triangles into a pleasing random arrangement. Sophia used 29 rows of 48 triangles each.

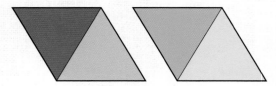

Join the triangles to form long strips, pressing the seams open.

Join long strips together offsetting triangles as shown in the diagram.

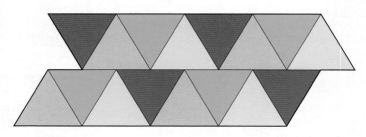

Denise's Details:
When you trim the side of a quilt that involves setting triangles or triangles like this quilt, try to use a long ruler and line up three points at a time.

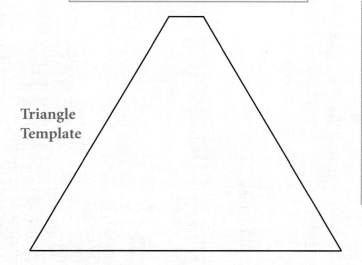

Triangle Template

BORDERS

Stay stitch the edges of the quilt from point to point. Trim the quilt edges 1/4" outside of the stay stitching.

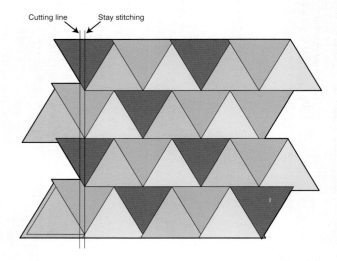

Cutting line   Stay stitching

Stitch the border strip together end to end.
Measure through the center of your quilt from top to bottom. Cut 2 border strips from the step above to this length and stitch to sides of quilt top.

Measure through the center of your quilt from side to side. Cut two borders strips to this length and add to the top and bottom of quilt top.

Quilt as desired and bind.

Denise's Details:
If you end up with a quilt that isn't square because of all the bias edges, take the time to measure through the top, middle and bottom of the quilt and take the average of the three measurements for your border. Then you can ease the quilt edges to fit the borders and your quilt will end up square.

Magnolia Branch Table Runner

17" X 52"

Made by Denise Sheehan, Lafayette, California
Quilted by Diana Johnson, San Leandro, California

I used an expanded version of the Magnolia Branch and the Garden Steps blocks from the Graceful Garden quilt to make this table runner featuring wool appliqué. The pastel colors make it ideal for a springtime dining table.

SUPPLIES

For blocks:
1/4 yard or 1 fat quarter blue
16 pieces at least 2 7/8" square assorted pink and green fabrics

For appliqué:
2/3 yard appliqué background fabric
fat quarters of green, blue, dark pink and pink wool

For borders:
1 3/8 yards if you are cutting from the length of the fabric as I did. If you are piecing your border and want to cut strips from the width of the fabric, you will need 1/2 yard.

Binding fabric: 1/2 yard

Backing: 1 1/4 yard

Embroidery Floss
pink and blue

Optional
Sulky 12-weight cotton thread to match wool colors

CUTTING

From the appliqué background fabric:
Cut 1 – 12 1/2"x 25" rectangle.
Cut 4 – 7 1/2" squares (these are oversized and will be trimmed down). Cut each of these once on the diagonal.

From the blue block background fabric:
Cut 16 – 2 7/8" squares. Cut each of these once diagonally.

From the assorted pinks and greens:
Cut 16 – 2 7/8" squares. Cut each of these once diagonally.
From the border fabric: (If you are cutting from the width of your fabric, cut 4 – 4" wide strips. Stitch the strips together end to end and cut the following from the long strip.)
Cut 2 – 4" x 47 1/2" rectangles.
Cut 2 – 4" x 19" rectangles.

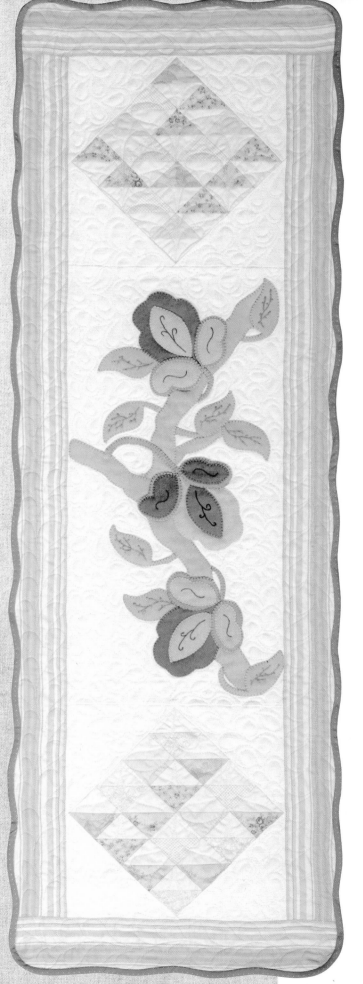

From the binding fabric:
Cut approximately 131" of 2 1/4" bias strips.

PIECING

Referring to page 41, make two Garden Steps blocks.

Finger press a background triangle to find the center of the long side. Match the triangle center to the center of Garden Steps side.

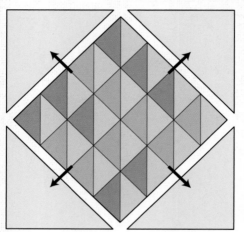

Stitch the triangles to opposite sides of each block. Add the remaining triangles as shown in the diagram. Square up each block to 12".

WOOL APPLIQUÉ

Templates are on pages 99-102. Trace the appliqué pieces onto the dull side of the freezer paper. Iron the freezer paper templates to the wool using a dry iron. Cut out the shapes following the edge of the freezer paper. There is no need to add a seam allowance. Trace embroidery lines onto wool pieces.

I use Roxanne's Glue Baste-It (see resources page 112.) to attach the wool to the background. You could also use pins. I used a matching color of Sulky 12-weight 100 percent cotton thread to stitch the appliqué by machine. I used a blanket stitch which could also be done by hand. For the embroidery, use a Lazy Daisy stitch for the tiny leaves and Outline stitch for everything else.

> *Denise's Details:*
> When transferring lines for embroidery, if you will be using a lazy daisy stitch, just mark dots where the stitch will go. The daisy stitch can be lazy and doesn't always sit perfectly!

ASSEMBLY

Trim the appliqué background to 12" x 24 1/2."
Stitch a pieced block on each end of the
appliqué block as shown in the diagram.

BORDERS

Stitch 4" x 47 1/2" rectangles to sides of table
runner.
Stitch 4" x 19" rectangles to ends of table runner.

SCALLOPS

Cut a piece of freezer paper the length of your table runner center. With a permanent marker, trace Scallop Templates B, C and Br as shown on the Border guide on page 104. (Trace B and C on the dull side of the freezer paper. Trace B on the shiny side of the freezer paper to get Br.) Cut out the freezer paper template on the lines. Line up the straight edge of the freezer paper with the border seam line and iron in place. Trace the scalloped edge. Depending on the length of your table runner before or after quilting, you may need to adjust the scallops slightly.

For the ends of the table runner, cut a piece of freezer paper the width of your table runner. Fold it in half and trace Template A on page 103. Follow the same procedure to trace onto the table runner. You may need to adjust a scallop and smooth out the corner circle to make it fit perfectly.

Denise's Details:
Tracing the scallops onto your table runner can be done before or after quilting. For example, if you plan to use a scallop design or have someone else do the quilting, trace before. If you are using an all-over quilting pattern, you can trace the scallop after.

QUILTING

Layer the backing, batting and top. Quilt as desired.

Trim the table runner following traced lines. Attach the bias-cut binding following the scalloped edges.

Vanity Chair

14" FINISHED BLOCK

Made and quilted by Denise Sheehan, Lafayette, California

I found this charming little vanity chair at a thrift store. The seat was worn and the chair needed a fresh coat of paint. I took the cushion apart and replaced the foam with a new 2" thick piece of foam cut to the size of the plywood base which is about 14 1/2" in diameter. If your chair is a different size, you may need to adjust the measurements. I was inspired by the Whirligig block and decided to make the block a little more intricate. The angles of this block complement the curls of the chair back and the circular seat.

SUPPLIES

1 fat quarter each of light brown, medium brown, dark brown small floral, dark brown medium floral, light blue, red and cream
18" square piece of fabric for backing
18" square of batting

CUTTING

From the medium brown fabric:
Cut 2 – 4 3/8" squares. Cut each of these once on the diagonal.
Cut 2 – 4 3/4" squares. Cut each of these twice on the diagonal.

From the light blue fabric:
Cut 4 – 4 3/8" squares.

From the light brown fabric:
Cut 4 – 4 3/8" squares.

From the dark brown small floral fabric:
Cut 2 – 4 3/4" squares. Cut each of these twice on the diagonal.

From the red fabric:
Cut 1 – 4 3/4" square. Cut this twice on the diagonal.

From the cream fabric:
Cut 1 – 4 3/4" square. Cut this twice on the diagonal.

From the dark brown medium floral fabric:
Cut 4 – 4 1/4" x 21" strips. This is to cover a 2" thick piece of foam. Adjust this measurement if your foam is a different thickness.

PIECING

Half-square triangles

Referring to the diagram on page 32, draw a diagonal line from corner to corner on the wrong side of the light brown squares. With right sides together, layer a light brown square on top of a light blue square.
(See diagram Step 1)
Stitch 1/4" from each side of the drawn line.
(Step 2)
Cut apart on the marked line. (Step 3)
Press towards the light brown. (Step 4) The half-square triangle units should measure 4" square. Repeat these instructions for a total of 4 – 4" half square triangles.

Quarter Square Triangle

Stitch a dark brown triangle to a medium brown triangle as shown in diagram. Press toward the arrows. Repeat for a total of four dark brown/medium brown triangles. Make another four medium brown/dark brown triangles (reverse the position of the two browns).

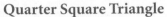

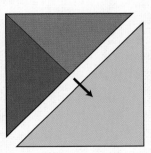

Stitch a light brown triangle to a dark brown/ medium brown unit. Repeat for a total of four of these units.

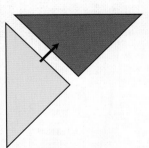

Stitch a red triangle to a cream triangle. Repeat for a total of four cream/ red triangles.

Stitch a blue triangle to a medium brown/dark brown unit. Repeat for a total of four of these units.

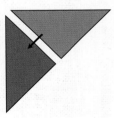

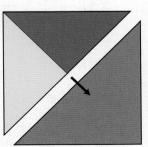

Stitch a medium brown triangle to a cream/red triangle. Repeat for a total of four of these units.

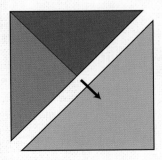

BLOCK ASSEMBLY

Arrange squares of the block as shown in diagram. Stitch the squares into rows.

Stitch the rows together.

QUILTING

Layer the backing, batting and quilt block.

Stitch in the ditch.

Trace a circle the same size as the base of your chair on the wrong side of quilt block. Stay stitch on this line to prevent stretching. Trim the block leaving a 3/8" seam allowance all around. Fold the circle in quarters and mark with pins.

SIDES

Stitch the dark brown medium floral strips together end to end so you have a circle of fabric. Zigzag the outer edge of the fabric to prevent raveling.

Machine baste 1/4" from the unfinished edge of fabric. Machine baste another row of stitches 1/8" outside the first row of stitches. Repeat on the zigzagged side.

Fold the circle of fabric in quarters and mark with pins.

With right sides together, using the unfinished side of the dark brown medium floral strip, pin the circle of fabric to the quilt block aligning pins on the quilt block circle and sides.

Pull up the basting stitches to take up extra fabric. Continue to pin the edges around the circle.

Stitch the top and sides together using a 3/8" seam allowance.

Center the quilt block on the foam and pin with straight pins to secure. Lay the wood circle on top of the foam. Pull up the basting stitches to fit the cushion/wood circle.

Staple edge of sides to the wood circle by placing one staple, pulling fabric taut, and stapling opposite side. Continue until entire edge has been stapled.

Attach the cushion to the chair and admire your handy work!

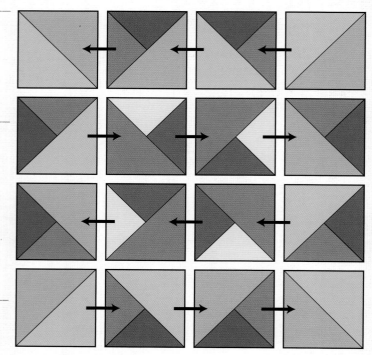

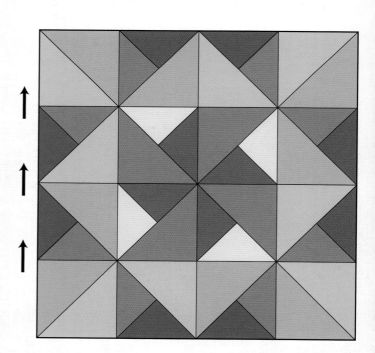

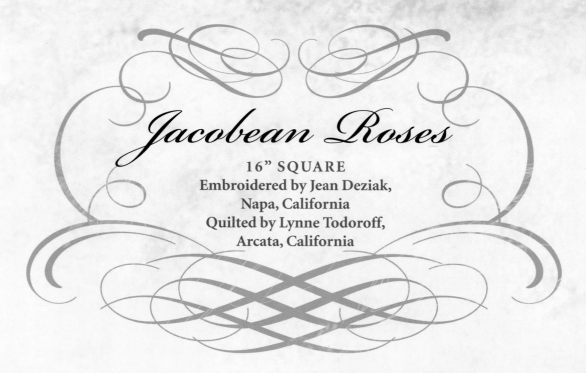

Jacobean Roses

16" SQUARE
Embroidered by Jean Deziak,
Napa, California
Quilted by Lynne Todoroff,
Arcata, California

Jean is a friend from the Morning Threads quilt group. This group was started over ten years ago as a drop in class by Verna Mosquera at our local quilt shop. Jean does beautiful embroidery and I was thrilled when she agreed to embroider The Rose block from The Graceful Garden quilt.

Think about how you want to use your project before cutting the background. After the project was complete, I decided it was so beautiful I wanted to frame it. It would have been easier if I had made the background a little bigger and thought about frame size first. My husband ended up cutting down a larger frame to fit the project. Jacobean Roses would also make a beautiful pillow.

SUPPLIES

1/2 yard cream or light tan background fabric
Several shades of pinks, green, brown and blue embroidery floss.
1/2 yard backing
18" square of batting

EMBROIDERY

The pattern is on pages 105-109.
Refer to the embroidery instructions on page 16. Trace lines from the pattern onto the background fabric. The center of the small flowers is a French Knot surrounded by small outline stitches. The tiny lines coming out of the center are straight stitches. All the other lines are stitched with a small outline stitch.

QUILTING

Lynne used YLI silk thread for the quilting (see resources on page 112.) to match the background. She echoed the motif and did a small stipple in the background.

Bind or frame if desired.

> *Denise's Details:*
> Floss from the Lecien Corporation was used to embroider Jacobean Roses (see resources page 112). The floss is cotton, but looks and feels like silk and needles well. If you choose to reproduce this project exactly as shown here, use the following COSMO colors:
> **Pinks:** 107, 205A, 2105, 240, 241A;
> **Greens:** 685, 989, 2535;
> **Browns:** 310, 312;
> **Blues:** 252, 253

D enise Sheehan has been quilting since 1997 when she took a class to make a postage stamp quilt (which is still waiting to be finished.) Her love for quilting skyrocketed at that point and she took classes on every technique and style of quilting. She has come full circle and now teaches quiltmaking.

Her pattern company, A Graceful Stitch was started in 2006 when the design side of quilting became her passion. Denise keeps her eyes open all the time, taking inspiration from what surrounds her. She likes to challenge herself with a variety of color palettes and a wide range of fabric choices. She tries to sew a little each day even if it's "after hours" when everyone else has gone to bed.

Denise lives in Lafayette, California with her husband and two daughters. Visit her website at www.agracefulstitch.com.

About the Author

49

50

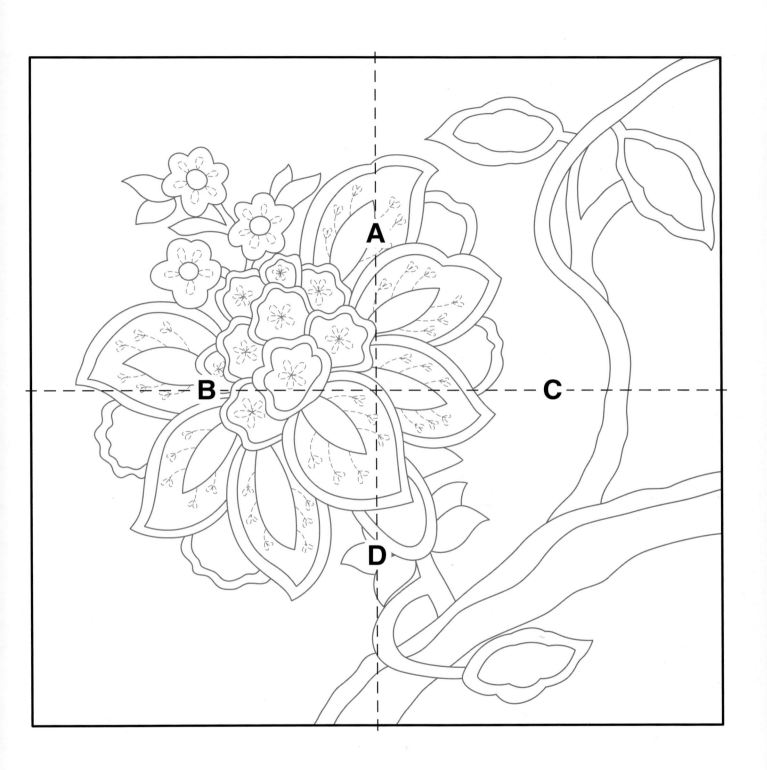

A

B   C

D

The Dahlia
BLOCK NO. 1 ASSEMBLY

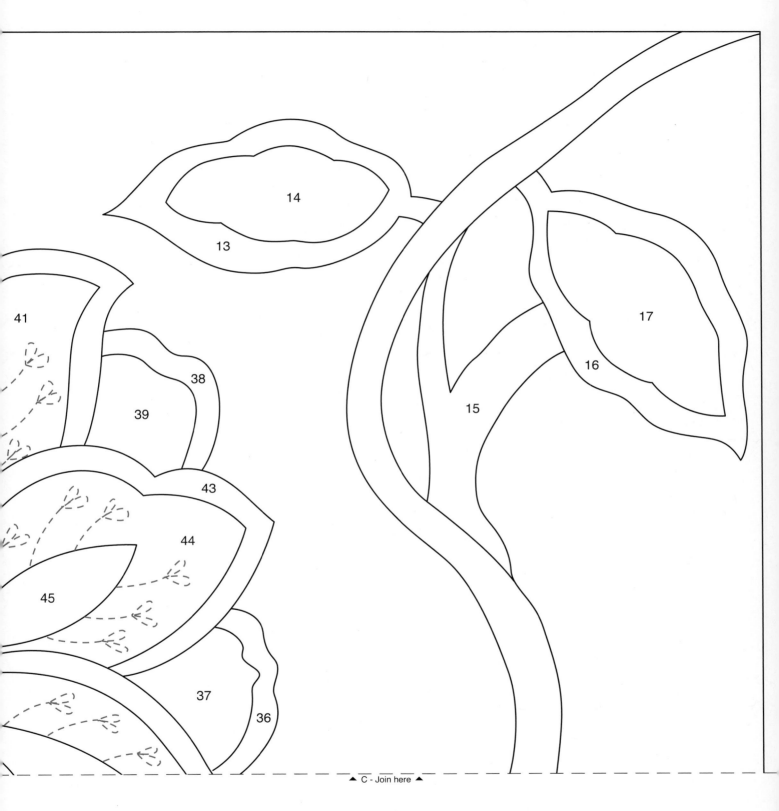

▲ C - Join here ▲

The Dahlia

BLOCK NO. 1 TEMPLATE 1-2

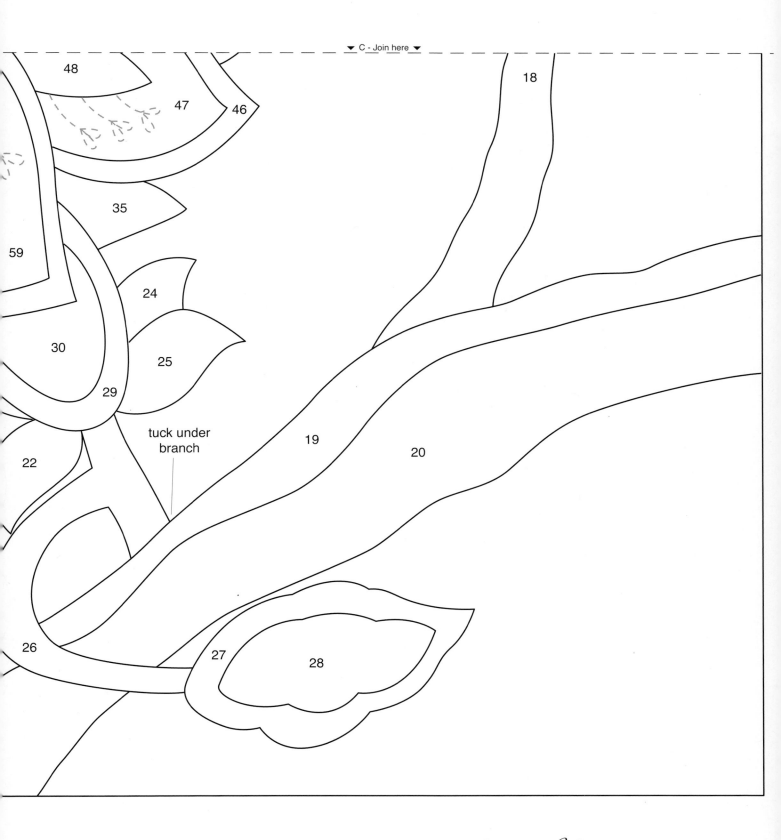

tuck under
branch

The Dahlia
BLOCK NO. 1 TEMPLATE 3-4

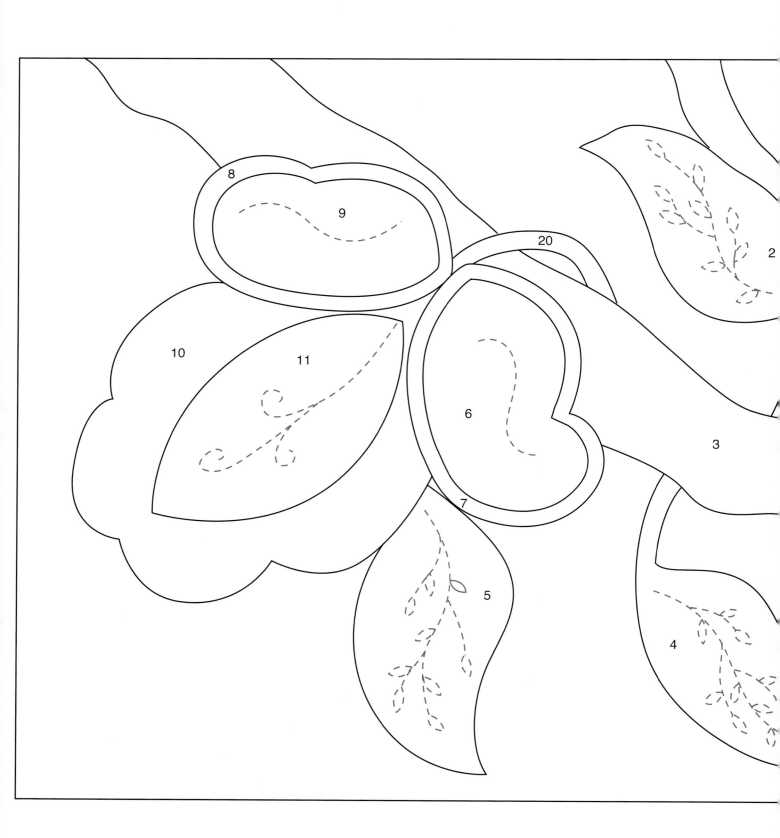

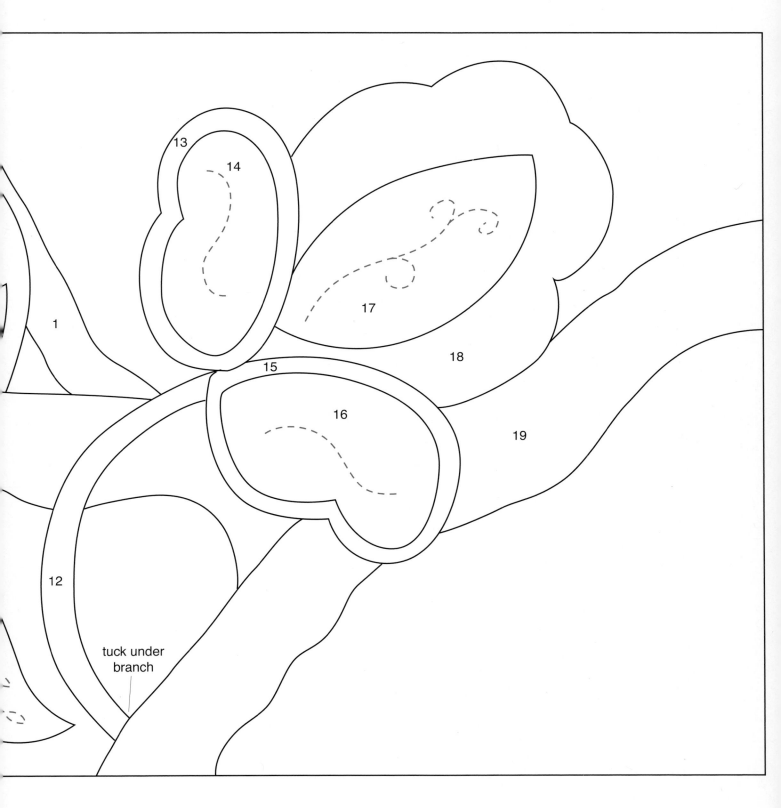

tuck under
branch

Magnolia Branch

BLOCK 5 TEMPLATE 1-2

The Poppy

BLOCK NO. 7 TEMPLATE

Poppy–
Mirror Image
BLOCK NO. 7 TEMPLATE

The Tulip

BLOCK NO. 8 TEMPLATE

The Iris
BLOCK NO. 10 TEMPLATE

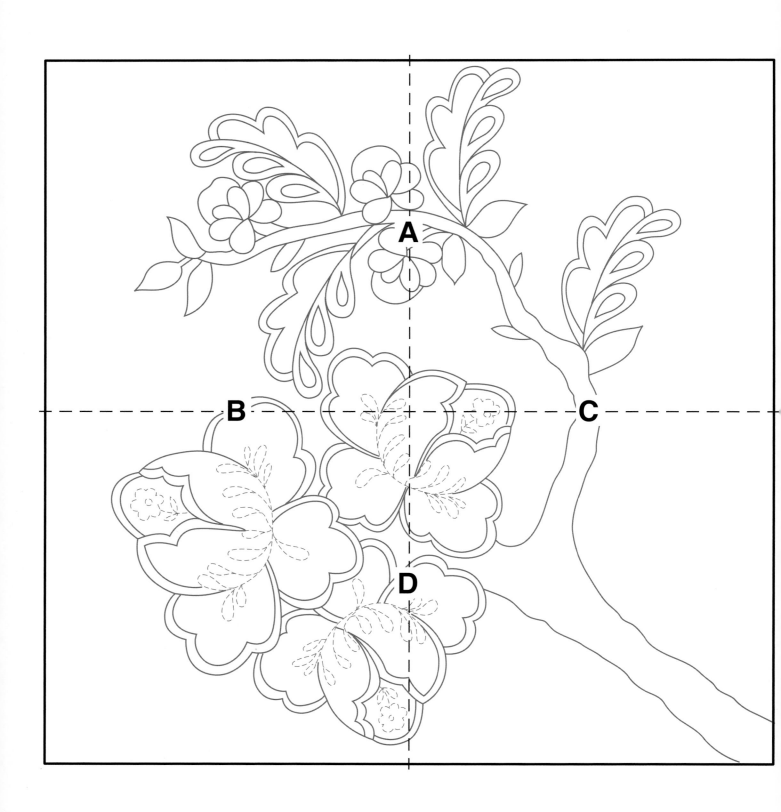

The Rose
ASSEMBLY DIAGRAM

The Rose

BLOCK NO. 12 TEMPLATE 1

The Rose

BLOCK NO. 12   TEMPLATE 2-3

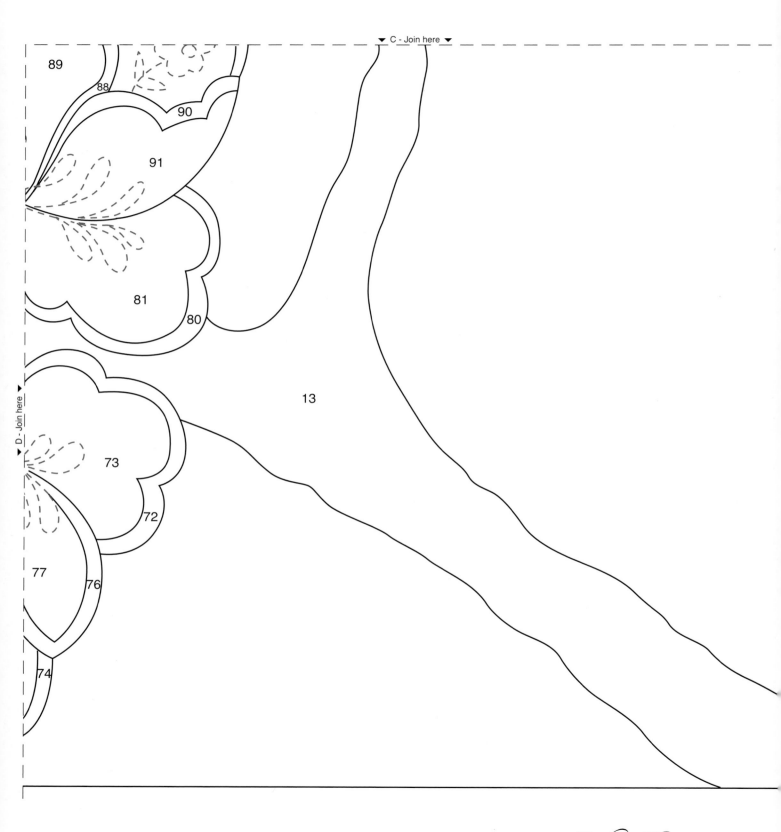

▼ C - Join here ▼

89

88

90

91

D - Join here ▶

81

80

13

73

72

77

76

74

The Rose

BLOCK NO. 12 TEMPLATE 4

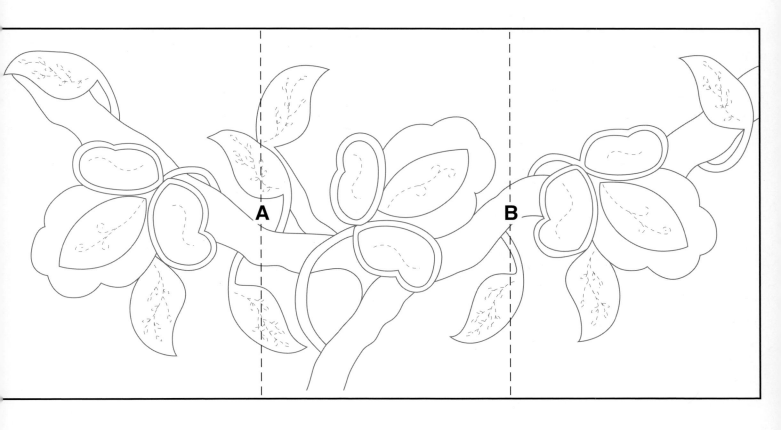

Magnolia Branch
Table Runner
ASSEMBLY DIAGRAM

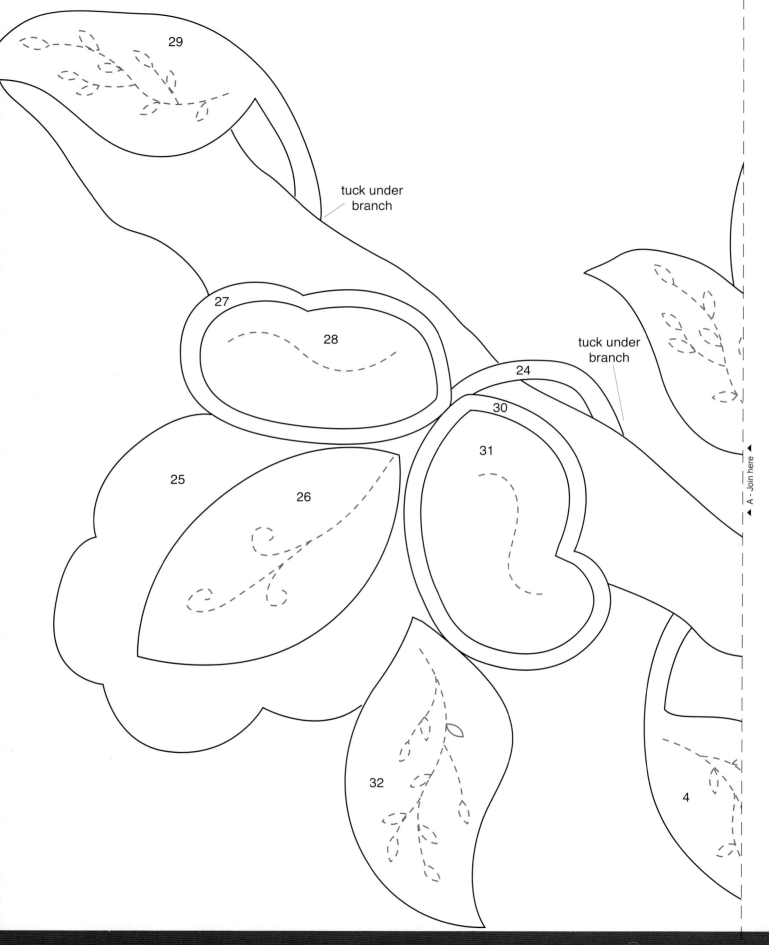

tuck under
branch

tuck under
branch

29

27

28

24

30

31

25

26

32

4

A - Join here

TEMPLATES

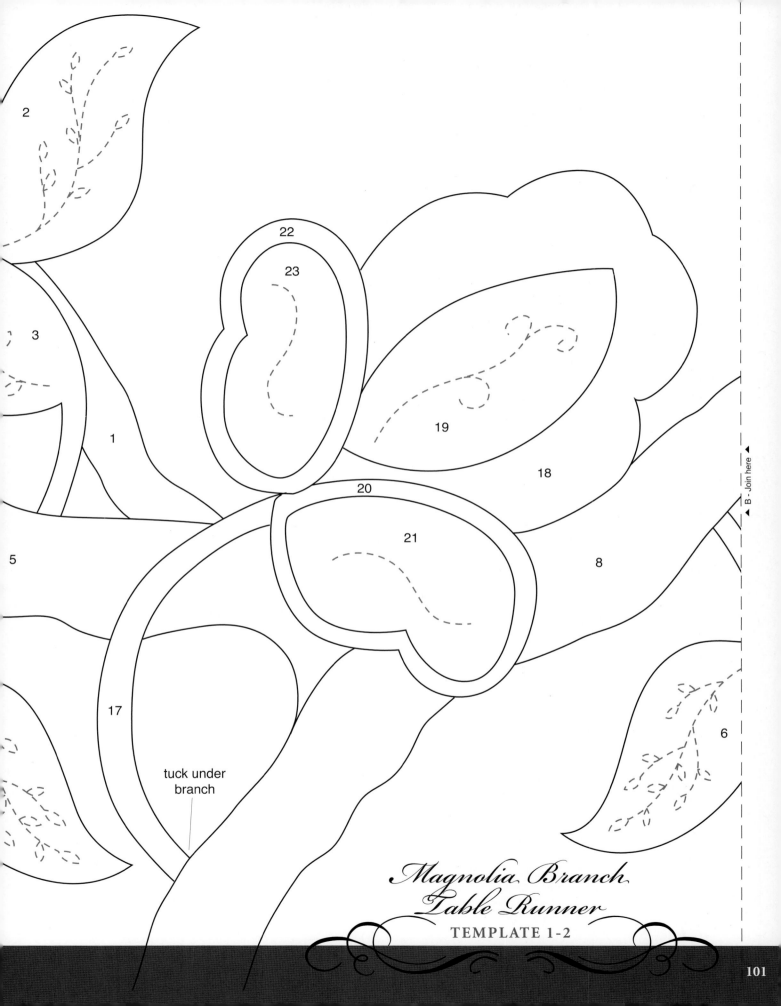

2

22

23

3

19

1

18

B - Join here ◄

5

20

21

8

17

6

tuck under
branch

Magnolia Branch
Table Runner
TEMPLATE 1-2

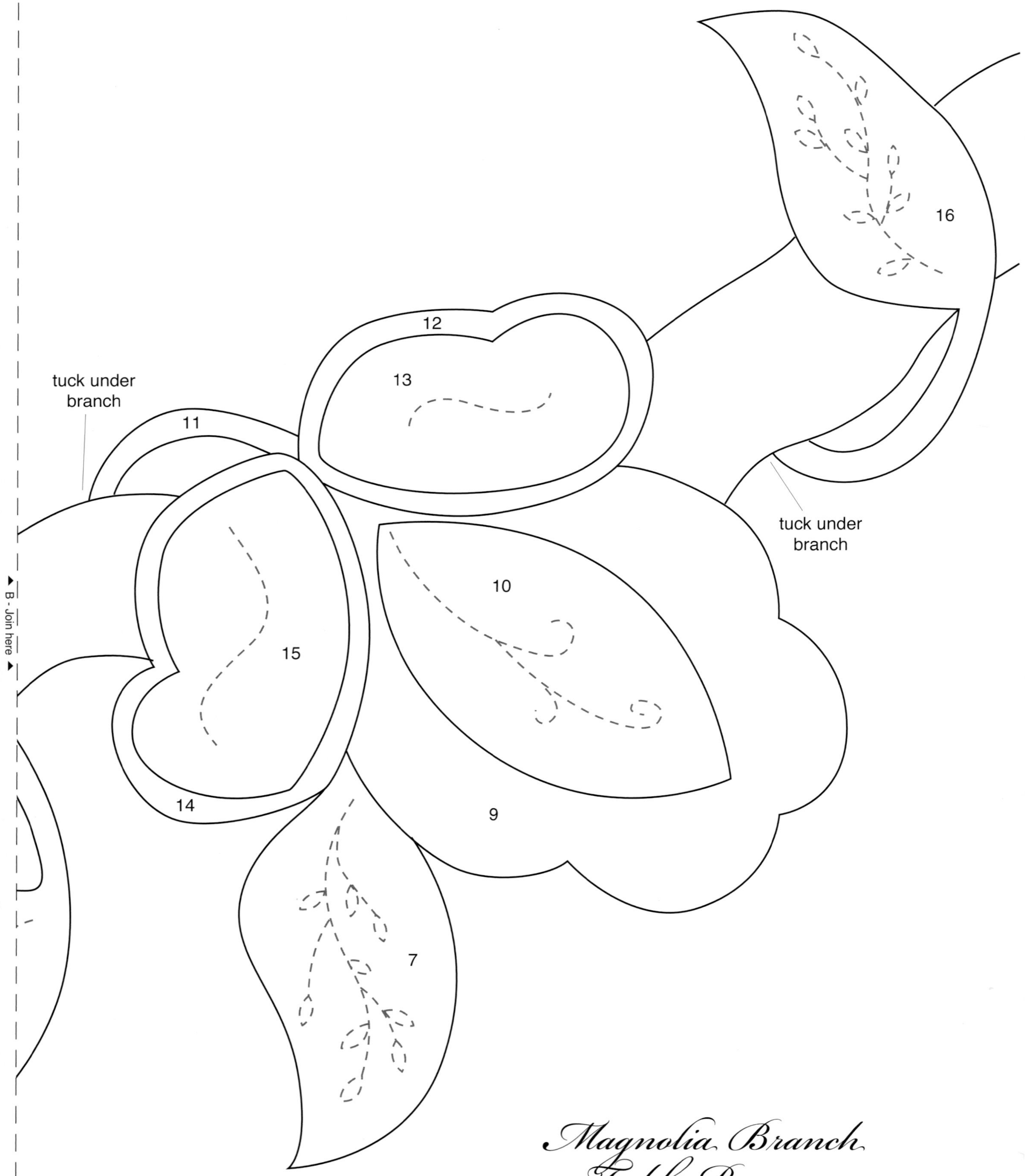

tuck under
branch

16

12

13

11

tuck under
branch

◄ B · Join here ►

10

15

9

14

7

Magnolia Branch
Table Runner
TEMPLATE 3

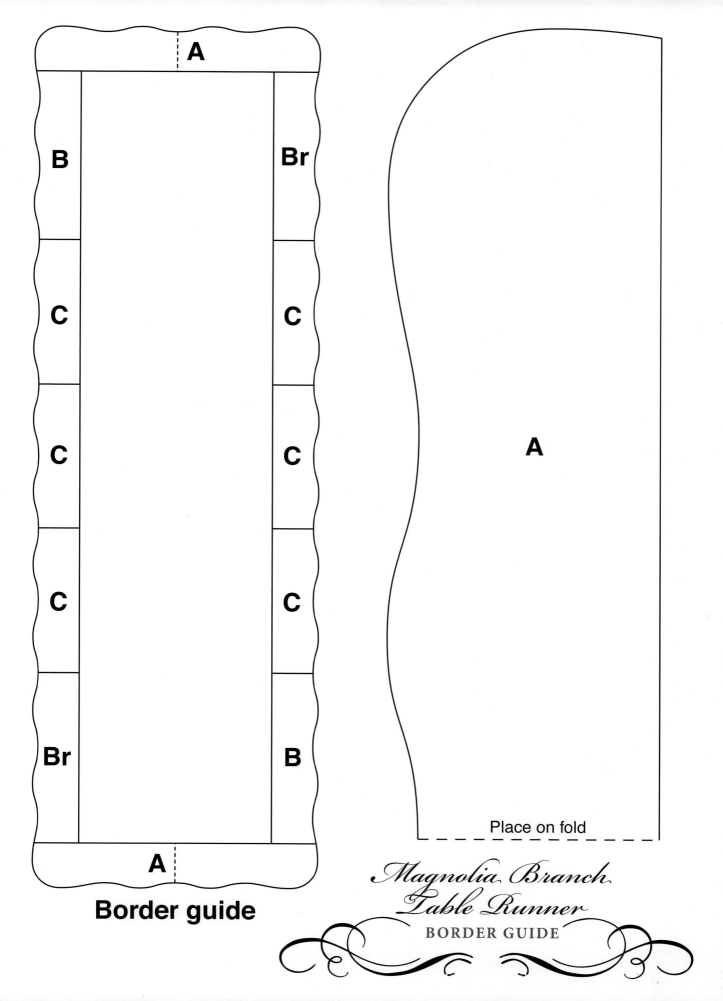

A

B

Br

C

C

C

C

C

C

C

C

Br

B

A

Border guide

A

Place on fold

Magnolia Branch
Table Runner
BORDER GUIDE

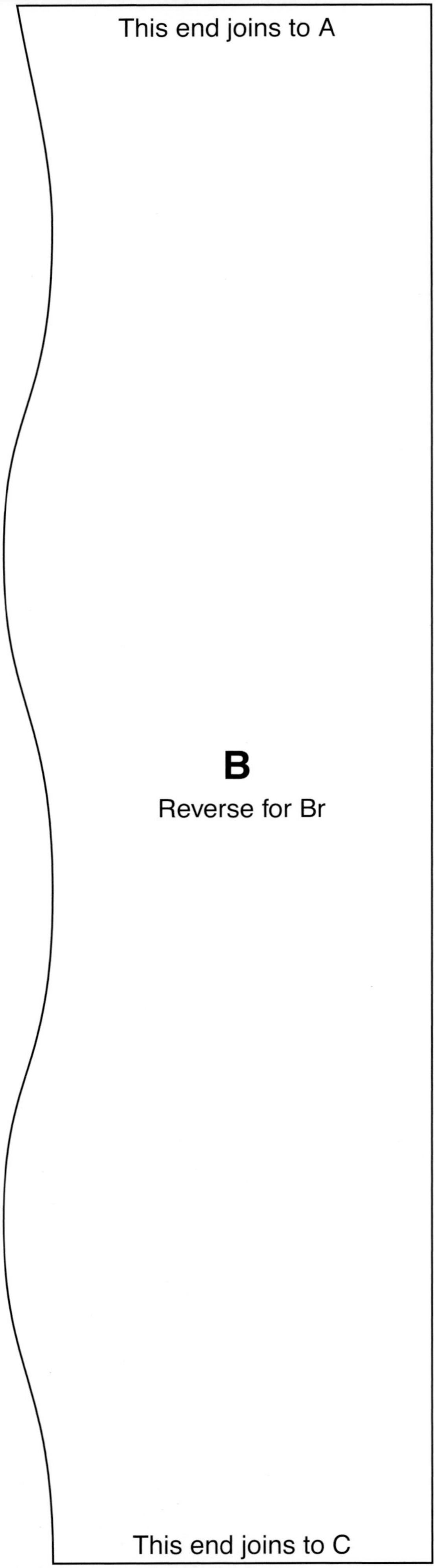

This end joins to A

B

Reverse for Br

This end joins to C

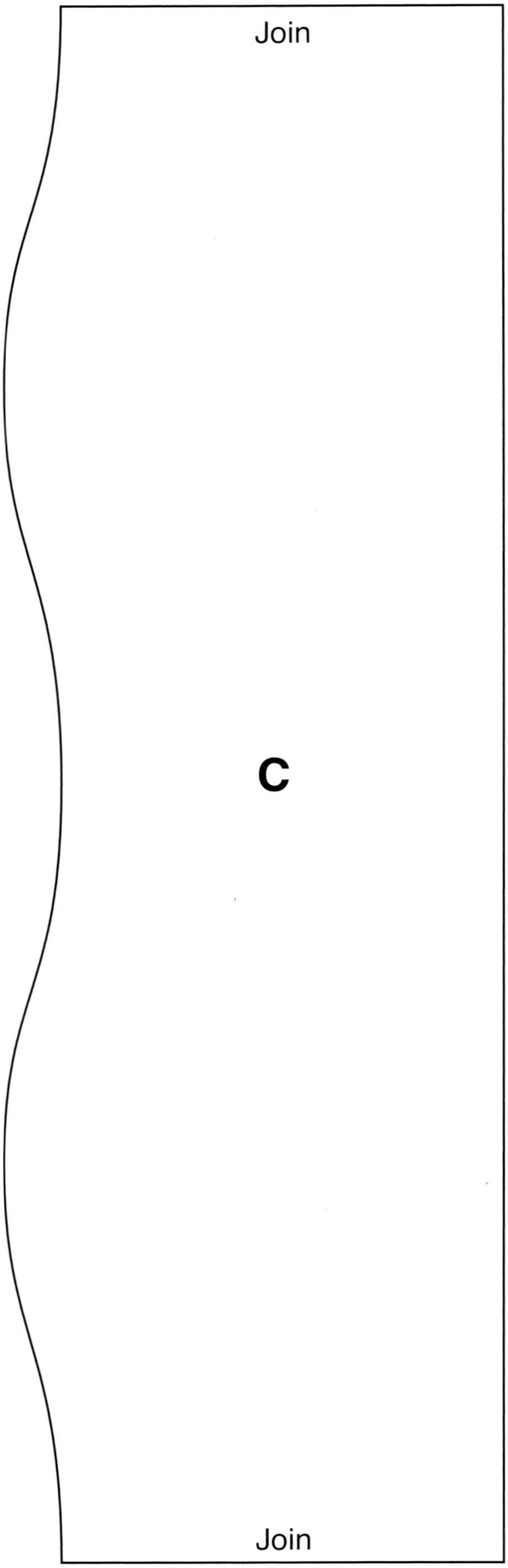

Join

C

Join

Magnolia Branch
Table Runner

BORDER TEMPLATES

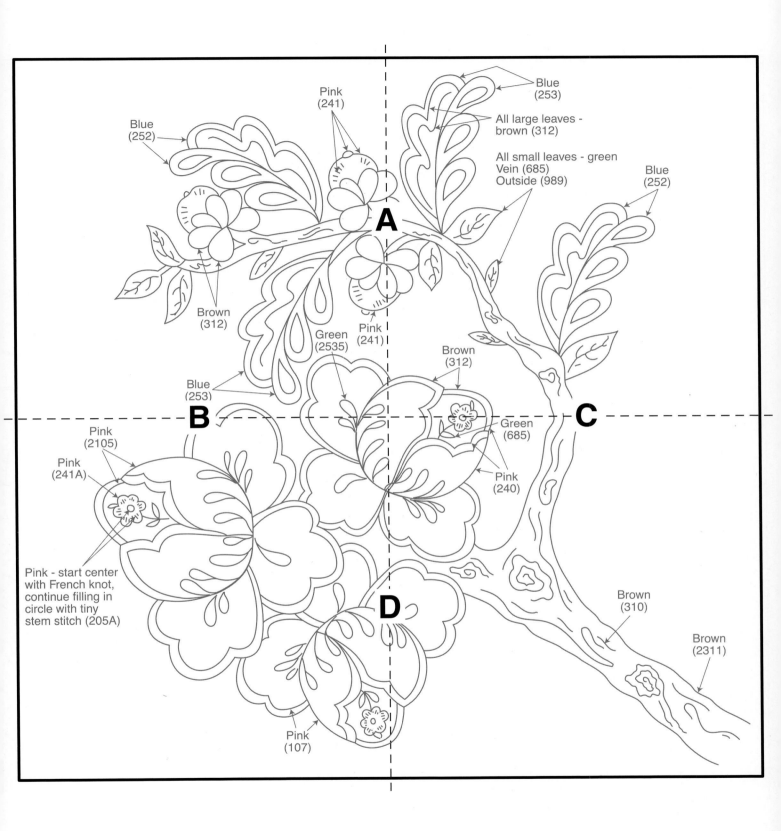

Pink (241)

Blue (252)

Blue (253)

All large leaves - brown (312)

All small leaves - green
Vein (685)
Outside (989)

Blue (252)

Brown (312)

Green (2535)

Pink (241)

Brown (312)

Blue (253)

A

Green (685)

C

Pink (2105)

Pink (240)

Pink (241A)

B

Pink - start center with French knot, continue filling in circle with tiny stem stitch (205A)

D

Brown (310)

Brown (2311)

Pink (107)

Jacobean Rose
ASSEMBLY DIAGRAM

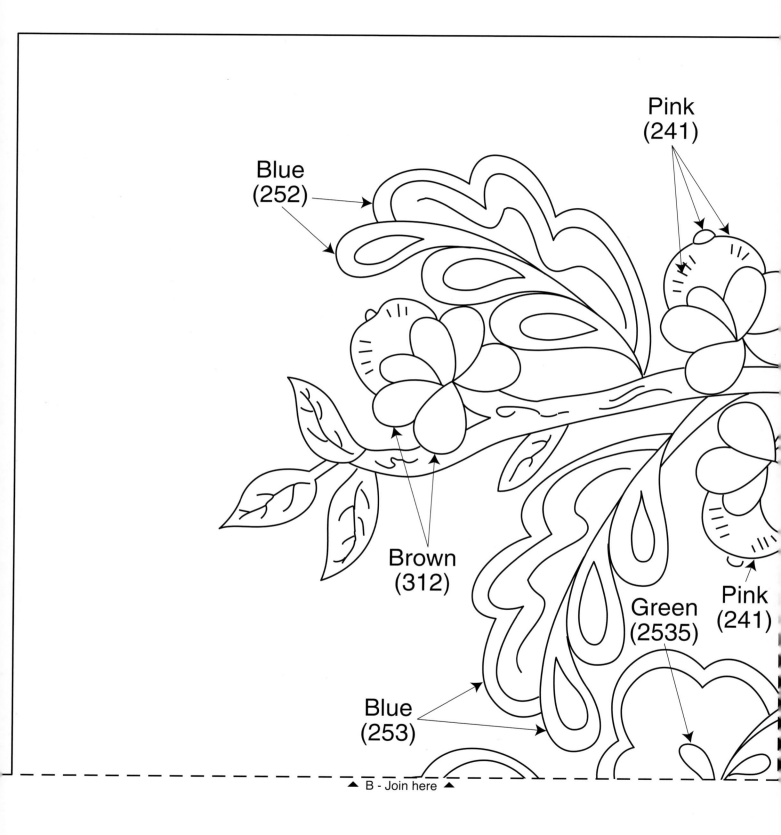

Blue
(252)

Pink
(241)

Brown
(312)

Green
(2535)

Pink
(241)

Blue
(253)

▲ B - Join here ▲

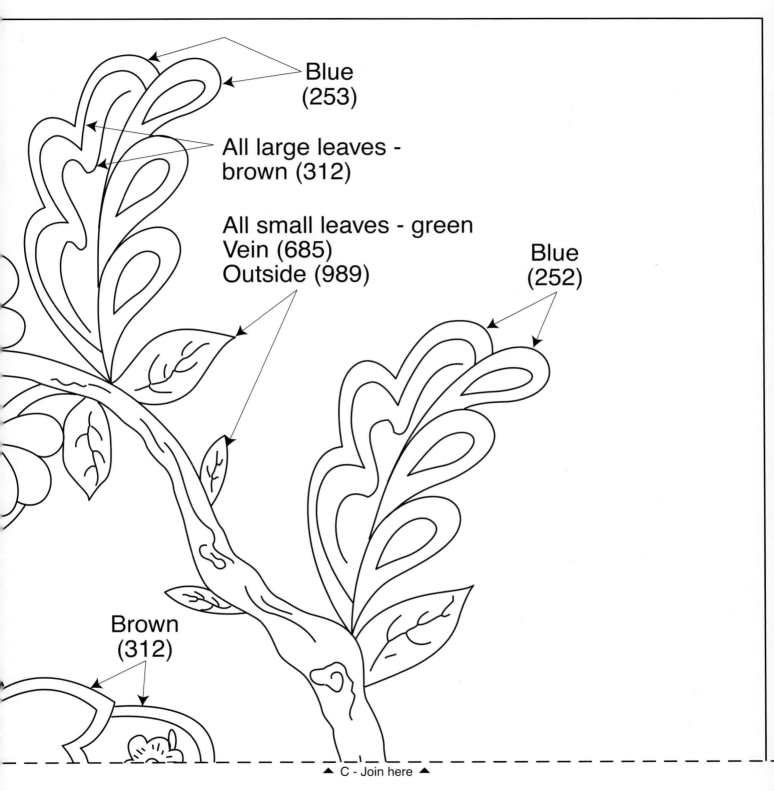

Blue
(253)

All large leaves -
brown (312)

All small leaves - green
Vein (685)
Outside (989)

Blue
(252)

Brown
(312)

▲ C - Join here ▲

Jacobean Rose
TEMPLATE 1-2

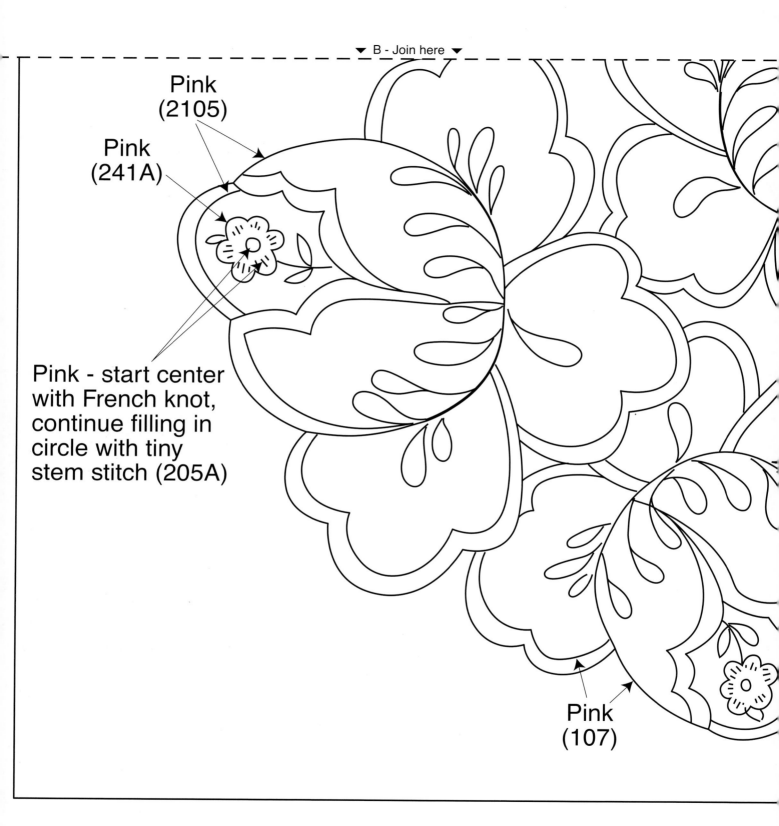

Pink
(2105)

Pink
(241A)

Pink - start center
with French knot,
continue filling in
circle with tiny
stem stitch (205A)

Pink
(107)

▼ C - Join here ▼

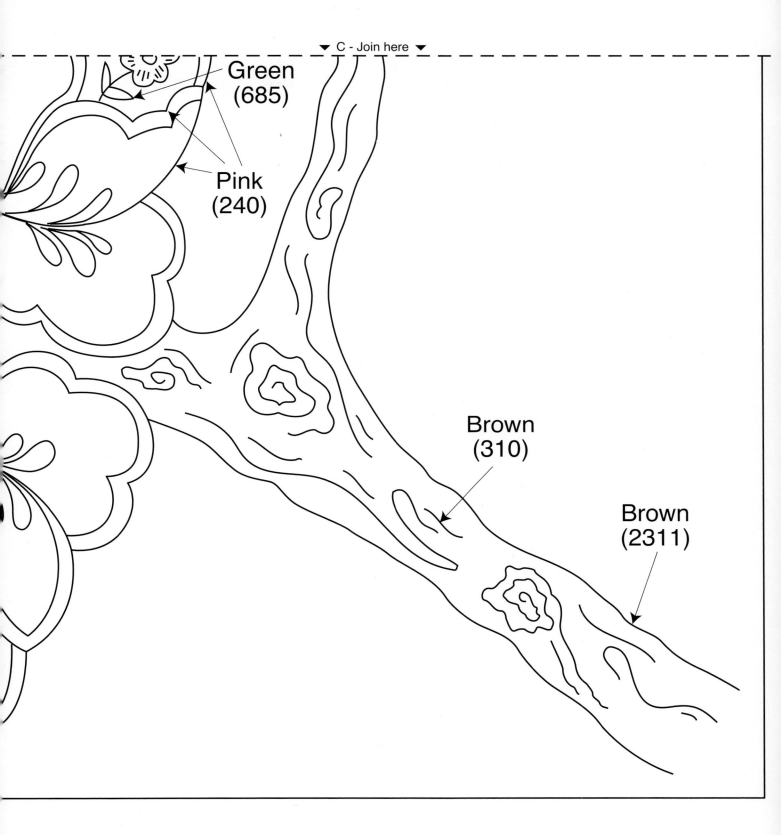

Green
(685)

Pink
(240)

Brown
(310)

Brown
(2311)

Jacobean Rose
TEMPLATE 3-4

One Piece at a Time by Kansas City Star Books – 1999

More Kansas City Star Quilts by Kansas City Star Books – 2000

Outside the Box: Hexagon Patterns from The Kansas City Star by Edie McGinnis – 2001

Prairie Flower: A Year on the Plains by Barbara Brackman – 2001

The Sister Blocks by Edie McGinnis – 2001

Kansas City Quiltmakers by Doug Worgul – 2001

O' Glory: Americana Quilts Blocks from The Kansas City Star by Edie McGinnis – 2001

Hearts and Flowers: Hand Appliqué from Start to Finish by Kathy Delaney – 2002

Roads and Curves Ahead: A Trip Through Time with Classic Kansas City Star Quilt Blocks by Edie McGinnis – 2002

Celebration of American Life: Appliqué Patterns Honoring a Nation and Its People by Barb Adams and Alma Allen – 2002

Women of Grace & Charm: A Quilting Tribute to the Women Who Served in World War II by Barb Adams and Alma Allen – 2003

A Heartland Album: More Techniques in Hand Appliqué by Kathy Delaney – 2003

Quilting a Poem: Designs Inspired by America's Poets by Frances Kite and Deb Rowden – 2003

Carolyn's Paper Pieced Garden: Patterns for Miniature and Full-Sized Quilts by Carolyn Cullinan McCormick – 2003

Friendships in Bloom: Round Robin Quilts by Marjorie Nelson and Rebecca Nelson-Zerfas – 2003

Baskets of Treasures: Designs Inspired by Life Along the River by Edie McGinnis – 2003

Heart & Home: Unique American Women and the Houses that Inspire by Kathy Schmitz – 2003

Women of Design: Quilts in the Newspaper by Barbara Brackman – 2004

The Basics: An Easy Guide to Beginning Quiltmaking by Kathy Delaney – 2004

Four Block Quilts: Echoes of History, Pieced Boldly & Appliquéd Freely by Terry Clothier Thompson – 2004

No Boundaries: Bringing Your Fabric Over the Edge by Edie McGinnis – 2004

Horn of Plenty for a New Century by Kathy Delaney – 2004

Quilting the Garden by Barb Adams and Alma Allen – 2004

Stars All Around Us: Quilts and Projects Inspired by a Beloved Symbol by Cherie Ralston – 2005

Quilters' Stories: Collecting History in the Heart of America by Deb Rowden – 2005

Libertyville: Where Liberty Dwells, There is My Country by Terry Clothier Thompson – 2005

Sparkling Jewels, Pearls of Wisdom by Edie McGinnis – 2005

Grapefruit Juice and Sugar: Bold Quilts Inspired by Grandmother's Legacy by Jenifer Dick – 2005

Home Sweet Home by Barb Adams and Alma Allen – 2005

Patterns of History: The Challenge Winners by Kathy Delaney – 2005

My Quilt Stories by Debra Rowden – 2005

Quilts in Red and Green and the Women Who Made Them by Nancy Hornback and Terry Clothier Thompson – 2006

Hard Times, Splendid Quilts: A 1930s Celebration, Paper Piecing from The Kansas City Star by Carolyn Cullinan McCormick – 2006

Art Nouveau Quilts for the 21st Century by Bea Oglesby – 2006

Designer Quilts: Great Projects from Moda's Best Fabric Artists – 2006

Birds of a Feather by Barb Adams and Alma Allen – 2006

Feedsacks! Beautiful Quilts from Humble Beginnings by Edie McGinnis – 2006

Kansas Spirit: Historical Quilt Blocks and the Saga of the Sunflower State by Jeanne Poore – 2006

Bold Improvisation: Searching for African-American Quilts – The Heffley Collection by Scott Heffley – 2007

The Soulful Art of African-American Quilts: Nineteen Bold, Improvisational Projects by Sonie Ruffin – 2007

Alphabet Quilts: Letters for All Ages by Bea Oglesby – 2007

Beyond the Basics: A Potpourri of Quiltmaking Techniques by Kathy Delaney – 2007

Golden's Journal: 20 Sampler Blocks Honoring Prairie Farm Life by Christina DeArmond, Eula Lang and Kaye Spitzli – 2007

Borderland in Butternut and Blue: A Sampler Quilt to Recall the Civil War Along the Kansas/Missouri Border by Barbara Brackman – 2007

Come to the Fair: Quilts that Celebrate State Fair Traditions by Edie McGinnis – 2007

Cotton and Wool: Miss Jump's Farewell by Linda Brannock – 2007

You're Invited! Quilts and Homes to Inspire by Barb Adams and Alma Allen, Blackbird Designs – 2007

Portable Patchwork: Who Says You Can't Take it With You? by Donna Thomas – 2008

Quilts for Rosie: Paper Piecing Patterns from the '40s by Carolyn Cullinan McCormick – 2008

Fruit Salad: Appliqué Designs for Delicious Quilts by Bea Oglesby – 2008

Red, Green and Beyond by Nancy Hornback and Terry Clothier Thompson – 2008

A Dusty Garden Grows by Terry Clothier Thompson – 2008

We Gather Together: A Harvest of Quilts by Jan Patek – 2008

With These Hands: 19th Century-Inspired Primitive Projects for Your Home by Maggie Bonanomi – 2008

As the Cold Wind Blows by Barb Adams and Alma Allen – 2008

Caring for Your Quilts: Textile Conservation, Repair and Storage by Hallye Bone – 2008

The Circuit Rider's Quilt: An Album Quilt Honoring a Beloved Minister by Jenifer Dick – 2008

Embroidered Quilts: From Hands and Hearts by Christina DeArmond, Eula Lang and Kaye Spitzli – 2008

Reminiscing: A Whimsicals Collections by Terri Degenkolb – 2008

Scraps and Shirttails: Reuse, Re-purpose and Recycle! The Art of Green Quilting by Bonnie Hunter – 2008

Flora Botanica: Quilts from the Spencer Museum of Art by Barbara Brackman – 2009

Making Memories: Simple Quilts from Cherished Clothing by Deb Rowden – 2009

Pots de Fleurs: A Garden of Applique Techniques by Kathy Delaney – 2009

Wedding Ring, Pickle Dish and More: Paper Piecing Curves by Carolyn McCormick - 2009

Queen Bees Mysteries:

Murders on Elderberry Road by Sally Goldenbaum – 2003

A Murder of Taste by Sally Goldenbaum – 2004

Murder on a Starry Night by Sally Goldenbaum – 2005

Dog-Gone Murder by Marnette Falley – 2008

Project Books:

Fan Quilt Memories by Jeanne Poore – 2000

Santa's Parade of Nursery Rhymes by Jeanne Poore – 2001

As the Crow Flies by Edie McGinnis – 2007

Sweet Inspirations by Pam Manning – 2007

Quilts Through the Camera's Eye by Terry Clothier Thompson – 2007

Louisa May Alcott: Quilts of Her Life, Her Work, Her Heart by Terry Clothier Thompson – 2008

The Lincoln Museum Quilt: A Reproduction for Abe's Frontier Cabin by Barbara Brackman and Deb Rowden – 2008

Dinosaurs - Stomp, Chomp and Roar by Pam Manning – 2008

Carrie Hall's Sampler: Favorite Blocks from a Classic Pattern Collection by Barbara Brackman – 2008

Just Desserts: Quick Quilts Using Pre-cut Fabrics by Edie McGinnis - 2009

DVD Projects:

The Kansas City Stars: A Quilting Legacy – 2008

Resources

Most of these products are available through your local quilt shop or by special order.

Appliqué supplies

Pearl P. Pereira Designs
768 Santa Barbara Drive
San Marcos, CA 92078
(760) 510-1832
(760) 510-3872 (Fax)
www.p3designs.com

YLI Silk Thread

Connecting Threads
13118 N.E. 4th St.,
Vancouver, Washington 98684
(360) 260-8900 fax (360) 260-8877
www.connectingthreads.com

COSMO Embroidery Thread

ThimbleCreek Quilt Shop
1150 D Burnett Ave.
Concord, Ca 94520
(925)676-5522
www.thimblecreek.com

Mary Ellen's Best Press Starch

Mary Ellen Products, Inc.
1-800-328-6294

Roxanne's Glue Baste-it

Roxanne International
742 Granite Avenue
Lathrop, CA 95330
Toll Free:1-800-993-4445
Fax: 209-983-8253

Aleene's OK to Wash It Glue

Duncan Enterprises
5673 E. Shields Avenue
Fresno, CA 93727
Toll-Free: 1-800-438-6226
Telephone: 559-291-4444
Fax: 559-291-9444

Jeana Kimball's Straw Needles

Foxglove Cottage
P.O. Box 220
Spring City, UT 84662
Phone: 435-462-9618
www.jeanakimballquilter.com

Freezer Paper

Grocery and Drug Stores
Reynolds Kitchens
6603 W. Broad Street
Richmond, VA 23230
800-433-2244

To see more of Denise's designs:
www.agracefulstitch.com